Standing in the Eye of the Storm

The true story of how a black woman breathed life into a broken white woman

Inspired by Stormy Nicole Wellington

By Kimberly Tocco

eBook published by Tenacious Productions
Copyright © 2024 All Rights Reserved

Believing is the Beginning

Faith is the Process

Knowing is the Result

This is a spiritual tale, one that will take you to places you may not be ready to go yet one that needs to be told. Buckle up butter cup, for tales are for the teller to tell and this one is a wild ride on the other side of what you think you know yet have no idea.

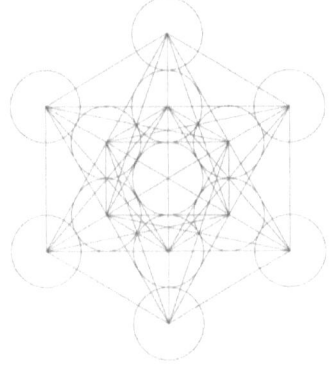

ENERGY IS EVERYTHING AND EVERYTHING IS ENERGY

Allow yourself to go on this journey with me, set aside what you believe, judge and understand and just ALLOW. *Tales are for the teller to tell and I am the teller of tales.*

"The student of spiritual psychology studies science as a form of devotion to Gad in the form of understanding the natural World." – THOTH

"The more I study science, the more I believe in God." – Albert Einstein

"Nothing in life is to be feared, it is to be understood." – Marie Curie

"The more I study nature, the more I stand amazed at the work of the creator. Science brings men closer to God." – Louis Pasteur

"I define God as an energy. A spiritual energy. It has no denomination, it has no judgment, it has an energy that when we're connected to it we know why we're here and what we're here to do." – Debbie Ford

"The first gulp from the glass of natural sciences will turn you into an atheist, but at the bottom of the glass God is waiting for you." – Werner Heisenberg

"…if humans only study the material elements, they can at best, discover but half the mystery."- The Secret Teachings of all Ages- Manly P. Hall

PREFACE

June 2021

Delphi Metaphysical University ~ 2nd visit and course in Advanced Channeling

We had been practicing deep meditation, these were bringing in strong visions for me of both past lives and messages. Like watching a shadowy black and white movie that had sound but muffled. I could make out some of the images and what was said. It takes practice to get things to come into focus and decipher what is manipulated by the mind and what is actually channeled from thy higher self. I had started to see a time in what appeared to be the Mayan Temples, long ago, I was inside dipping a vase into the waters than ran through the Temple and taking them to wash the feet of Queens. It was an extremely high honor and position to have, a priestess giving the blessing of clearing energy of the DNA of those Queens. The WAY SHOWERS, using the language of the Kings wearing a crown of flowers and delivering them unto their divine feminine power.

This will be the coming of a New Era to blanket the Earth for the Universe is feminine and she is calling back her voice, calling back her blood. Look for the dragons, look for the feathers.

I had no idea what this meant but it was so REAL to me. The next mediation, the messages came in even stronger, and I wrote down every word.

Do not lose faith little one, stop playing small, embrace who you are, embrace your light, walk in your regal self, let go of the things that distract. We will care for you; we will be with you and help you. It's OK to show the World without saying anything of who you truly are. Your gifts are ready to emerge, you must open the door and call unto you the Great One who will support you and this path. You are whom you always believed and it's not that you are better than others, you have KNOWLEDGE that needs to be shared. Take the time to learn and develop and be selfish for you have gifts unto which the World will benefit only if you ALLOW yourself to come into you. STOP PLAYING SMALL

I was a little shook, I had many gifts, as we all do, and they had been growing strong for the last few years. Like much of the planet, covid had sent us into a shift in which our very DNA was becoming ignited to also shift and become a version of ourselves that needed to emerge in order to save humanity from what seems to be our final downfall. The next mediation I did showed me something I was not prepared for and even after I wrote down what was told to me and sketched the image that was shown, I was left confused.

This journey is for the own self. Speak for you and no one else. There is nothing you need. The memories are of the lessons learned. Like a child now off on her own, you must fly the coop. Spread your wings, nothing else matters if you just take care of you, listen, voice, write and what comes of that creates a vibration that has not been here upon the Earth as of yet. Orion was lost because you used all your energy and wisdom to try and fix everyone else. Fix YOU and others will naturally follow. Walk YOUR truth and all will be revealed. You do not need to fixate on being a leader and saving the World. We only need you to save yourself. The point of all of this is to show you that you only need to care for yourself this time. Naturally you will through the works of healing thyself. Elijah spoke and he asks that you step each step as the Queen you are, the sophisticated, beautiful ancient knowledge of who you are. The ripple effect of this will affect the past present and future. For Jason yes, but all others for whom are deeply connected. Stay calm, stay focused, observe, be pensive, have joy yes but do not give in to "small" of the past and hold the position of who you are. It is not arrogant; it is taking your place amongst the Kings. To love and be a servant of knowledge and peace. LEAD WITH THE LEADERS FOR IT IS THOSE LEADING IN LOVE WHO WILL BE CHOSEN BY THE PEOPLE FOR THE PEOPLE.

While this all sounded fantastic, I had no idea what it meant for I was just me, an ordinary girl who was trying her best to become extraordinary and who had failed at a lot of things, and achieved a great many things but I certainly was no "King". I started studying books I found at the University. Thoth, Ma'at, The Kabbala, Hermetic Principles, Freemasons, the Brotherhood of light, The Keys of Enoch, Elijah, for in order to understand the path in which we are going we must study the place in which we came. These writings felt so familiar, and I drank them in like water. As I studied, I discovered the image I saw mated one that was common in all of these writings.

The All-Seeing Eye! Still, I had no idea what to do with all of this besides to continue to study and try and make connections and grow in my confidence. I closed my journal I had made those notes in and shoved it into a drawer when I returned home, not to pull it out again…

UNTIL DECEMBER OF 2022

…I saw her on stage after judging the Great American Speak Off. This was the woman everyone had been talking about during the competition, one I had seen on social media, beautiful, powerful, exotic and free willed. I had listened to her while she made comments to the contestants, her voice was unusual and very different to me in person.

Her very presence was very different in person, I walked over and shook her hand and looked into her eyes.

FIRST LEADER, GREAT ONE, WOMAN KING

It was the same voice from my mediation all that time ago and I also saw myself washing her feet on a ship, an old ship from many centuries ago.

I had found her, THE VOICE who would lead many from despair and create the frequency which, as of yet…had not been seen on this planet.

Table of Content

- Preface
- Forward
- Dedications
- Chapter I Broken
- Chapter II The Storm
- Chapter III Thunder & Lightening
- Chapter IV The Sun broke through the Clouds
- Chapter V Turbulence
- Chapter VI Here comes the Storm
- Chapter VII Hurricane
- Chapter VIII Standing in the Eye of the Storm

FORWARD

Grief is Love with no place to go

…so, we rebirth ourself to build a legacy with the ripple effect of that love

…otherwise, you die in the suffering of your soul without purpose or passion

PASSION: derived from the Latin word *passio* meaning suffering OR a strong feeling enthusiasm or excitement for something. ie: The Passion of the Christ

Passion, yes, we LIVE for the passion and the curiosity of where it will take us, expand us and bring us closer to the ecstasy of being human. Yet passion doesn't have to come from a romance or inaction with a person. It is the sublime call to purpose, the feeling you get when you create, you're your imagination and it comes to life. Passion is born from a place deep within the heart, a place that bubbles up to the surface when we are drowning in our grief, our pain, our suffering. It is the cry of purpose which is usually triggered by a major sledgehammer in life. Humanities greatest philanthropic movements have been born from her deepest sorrows because we become PASSIONATE about the legacy we build from our grief and the legacy fueled by the love with no place to go

Thirteen years ago, on a random Tuesday morning getting my four sons fed and ready for school, my second born, thirteen-year-old Jason got into an argument with me over breakfast. Now mind you, this boy was a fantastic kid. Six foot one, could pitch at eighty miles per hour, a straight A student and one of the most popular at school. He was obviously going through the typical teenage "angst" and had been mouthy, but we had never seen him like this. After his father told him to go upstairs and wait for him to get back from his meeting instead of going to school because they needed to talk, Jason looked at me and said, "I hate you!"

Something I had never heard him say and again, a teenager so I looked at him and said," Yeah well, I hate you too. Go upstairs and wait for your father."

Shortly after, my entire World would crumble and fall as I would find my son laying on his left side, a hole in his head and a gun in his hand. I tried to work on him and keep him alive as I waited for the ambulance to arrive, but as I pumped his chest and breathed into his lungs, I felt him slowly die and leave his body.

…those last words to my son

…I too died that day

Grief is just love with no place to go and I had to find a place to put it. I had to change the foundation of suicide my son left behind into one of life. I had to transmute this horror and suffering into purpose.

"If you lose your wealth, you have lost nothing; if you lose your health, you have lost something; but if you lose your character, you have lost everything." – Woodrow Wilson

The soul writes the character yet it's the song within your heart that defines it.

I had lost my character holding my son and feeling his soul leave his body, I no longer could hear the song in my heart. A decade after that horrible day I had achieved incredible feats in my son's name, transmuted much of the trauma yet, I still had not found myself. I had to find my passion and curiosity to keep choosing ME and this is the story of how Stormy Wellington breathed life back into my broken wings and helped me fly again.

DEDICATIONS

Stormy Nicole Wellington, The Voice of the broken hearted, there are no words to express my gratitude, so I put it into my WORKS. You hold a piece of all of us within in you and we can feel the transmutation of our suffering through your magical soul. The burden of what you hold on your shoulders is great and I can only hope that I may have a ripple effect unto the World and do my part to bring you energy, joy and love.

In her words:

"I will hear the voice of the Holy Spirit Within

I will lead and not follow

I will create and not destroy

I am a force for good

I defy the odds

I set new standards

I am a leader

I am the head and not the tail

I am above and not beneath

I am the lender and not the barrower

I am loved by God

I am chosen by God

I am protected by God
No weapon formed against me shall prosper
Every tongue that rise up against shall be condemned"

Adversity advances the assignment, pass the test to your abundance, pressure is a privilege

"I AM IN A CONSTANT STATE OF ATTRACTING ALL THE GOOD I DESERVE AND I DESIRE"
- Stormy Wellington THE VOICE

…thank you for reminding me who I AM
Sheila Jones-Woodward, the prophetic eye, the voice of reason, the seller of VISIONS. Thank you for SEEING me, holding my hand when I felt weak and allowing me to break down and build myself back up with your words of wisdom.

My children, Brian, Giuseppe, Peter, and of course my Jason who lives in heaven. Your momma has a dream and I love you all so very much. Thank you for your patience and understanding as I navigated my way through these last few years. My Sons, there are no words except for these:

I am honored that you chose me to guide you in this lifetime and that you chose me to break our ancestorial traumas. I will accomplish the extraordinary for I am CHOSEN.

Peter my husband…we have had some HUGE ups and downs, yet we are still holding it together. Somehow, we always make it through, lovingly and respectfully. Let's keep going.

I do not back down

I do not give up

Keep Moving Forward

We may be broken yet we remain unbreakable

"The one thing that has brought me to my goals is my TENACITY"

– Kimberly Tocco AKA Tenacious T

The heart must break so the light can escape. Your soul has a purpose in the life, and that purpose is buried deep within the God Spark heart cells. Science has proven our heart cells have memory just as the brain. Pain is inevitable in this life because it is through pain that we can begin to take up the process of finding that buried treasure. This is what makes it a great adventure, this is what makes it a beautiful love story. The greatest love affair you can have is with the person in the mirror and life will test that love over and over again. Will you love yourself enough to keep pushing through no matter how painful the sledgehammers? Will you choose life and step out of suffering?

Take my hand, let the hunt for joy begin…

Chapter I
The Broken

Watching my child die in my arms, his body reflexing in his last breath, trying to comprehend what was happening, trying to understand that he took my gun that I hid under the mattress put it to his head and pulled the trigger...

I too, died that day

The minutes, hours, days, weeks, months and years that would follow are nothing short of a fiery hell and I had to find a way to crawl out of that pit of despair or forever burn in the suffering of that moment. The guilt of the last words I spoke to my son, the inability to see, as his mother who should have known, the failure to protect my child from harm. Thinking things like this would not happen to me. It ate away at me, festering and oozing within my very soul until all I could see was a thick fog of grief and the glass of wine in my hand. I would gather myself just enough throughout the day to be a mother to my remaining children, one of which had autism so multiple therapies throughout the day but for lunch I would have that glass of wine and by diner I was opening a second bottle.

Dull the pain
Dull the suffering
Dull the guilt
...dull the self-hatred

On top of the suffering of losing my child, I would come to also face the stigma of suicide. The trolls on social media, parents did not want their kids to come over to our house anymore.

Unlike losing a child to cancer, murder or accident, suicide whispers its dark voice of, *"What really happened in that house?"* and *"I bet it was Brian who shot him."*

Brian is my first born, 12 months older than his brother Jason yet in the same grade together. Brian was 14, Jason 13 and I also have twins Joey and Petey, age 3 at the time

I would receive memes of Jason with a target on his head and a gun in his hand. Mothers would stare and speak in low voices in rooms where I had to show up for school or counsel meetings for Brian. These whispers swirled like a toxic cloud over our heads. I would try to go to school functions for Brian's sake and we did give a good handful of friends who did not judge, just mourned with us. We came together and started a baseball charity as Jason loved baseball and we all wanted some way to keep him alive in our minds. He had such a talent when it came to sports being six foot one at thirteen, he could pitch at 80mph. Collect gently used equipment and funds to assist inner city kids and programs called Jason's Propulsion League. The older boys had been in 8th grade when Jason took his life and so starting high school without his brother was extremely difficult. I continued to show up at his school and it was one night at a football game that a student's mother walked up to me, as if in sympathy and asked a question that would shake me to the core of what was left of my shattered self. She was the mother of the first girl Jason found himself liking. They had sat together in the last class of the day and her daughter was deeply affected by his loss.

"Hi there, I was so sorry to hear about Jason. I thought I would approach you as my daughter was close to Jason. I just want you to ask you if Jason embraced Jesus?", she said standing in front of me with a superior attitude, looking down on me

"…umm I. I, we had all gone to church, he was baptized in our Catholic church when he was young." I stumbled over my words because I had not given this a thought. All I could do was try and wake up each day, push through it and then try and get some sleep when night came. The only way I could sleep even a few hours was drinking enough wine at night to soften the image of my son gagging and gurgling out his last breath.

"Well, I hope he did because he is going to burn in hell forever for what he did."

WHAT
WWHHAAAT!

In that instant I felt an anger drive through my gut like a hot poker.

"Excuse me? MY SON NEVER EVEN GOT A CHANCE TO KISS A GIRL LET ALONE SIN AND DESERVE HELL. HOW DARE YOU SAY THAT TO ME!"

I quickly turned and walked away as I was not sure what I would do to her the way I was feeling. I also did not want her to see the tears as they had already began streaming down my face. How could she say such a thing? Later that night I would start researching suicide, the statistics, the origins of why people had come to believe that it was the worst sin imaginable. I found that the church in its formation had taught that taking your own life meant such disrespect to God that the punishment would be the most severe. The fear of the punishment and burning for eternity connected to taking one's life can be traced back very early Christianity. The impoverished people began to take their life rather than to suffer the hard life they found themselves in under that kind of rule. To prevent the people from making that choice, it became known by the church as one of the worst sins and deserving of the eternal fire. By that logic, an impulsive choice made by a child of God made under the harsh conditions of this life you will now face eternity of damnation. I do not think so. To think that God would teach that if you chose in those moments to leave, you would receive a punishment from God even more severe than murder, pedophilia, adultery and rape is not my God. This is how they maintained the population working and tithing by instilling fear in them; the fear of the rath of God. I refused to believe my beautiful boy was trapped in a limbo of fire and brimstone. I refused to accept that God was anything other than a loving God. He was a child; he made an impulsive decision in a moment of feeling trapped with no place to turn. This stigma of suicide and assumed mental illness surrounding those who speak up about it has made it almost impossible for anyone to come forward and try to express what they themselves do not understand.

The 2022 statistics reported by the **CDC** *and* **WHO** *stated 13.2 million seriously think about doing it, 3.8 million make a plan and 1.7 million attempt suicide annually in the United States.*
...and those numbers are just the attempts not the death rate numbers

Since the early 2000's middle-aged women taking their life has increased 82% in America **(Maxwell School of Citizenship and Public affairs)**
Globally over 800,000 are lost to suicide each year **(2021 World Health Organization)**
Men account for 75% of all those because of the more lethal means used to complete the act and the LEADING cause of death **(2021 Mental Health Foundation)**

How is it this many people are sitting in a state of suffering and yet we still consider it a mental illness and a horrible sin? The reality is those numbers are increasing and we must remember that these are only the one reported. How many more have thought, planned or attempted? If we do not open the door to make it safe to discuss and work through, if we offer no solution then who really is to blame? If a child goes to their school counselor and expresses these thoughts, it's a mandatory 72 hour lock up and observation. I thought of my Jason, a pitcher, how much he loved playing baseball yet if he went to his coach, his coach would have probably benched him worried that it would be to much pressure. The I thought of that last day, how he was so off, and said those words of hate. Even if he would have expressed to us that he wanted to end his life, I would have blown it off and said to him, "Oh come on! You are a talented, handsome kid, popular and smart. Get it together, what do you have to complain about." I would not have taken him seriously because of his age and the facts that I didn't see a reason for him to be suffering. He had shown no signs of any emotional issues, he was a bit moody like any teenager but certainly not dark and depressed. He was six foot one and pitching no hitters, most popular kid in school what issues could he possibly have

With that one statement, I answered my own question. "What issues could he possibly have?" I had never asked him; not once did I sit down and just ask him or talk about this with him. The classic, "That will never happen to me." Delusional. That was the most difficult part of myself to face, the mother that failed to protect her child.

People hide behind forced smiles and fake profiles because they just want to find a place to belong, a safe place to open up and be authentic.
Suicide is free will, staring back at you, asking you to choose. If in that moment you are in your darkest hour, you will choose to leave this world.
Unless you pause. That is what I found I had to do. It's the pause prior to pulling the trigger, prior to swallowing the pills, prior to driving off that cliff, prior to kicking the chair out from under you and swinging from that rope. I had been there you see, many times. As I researched to try and understand my son's choice, I also remembered the first time I had thought of taking my life at seventeen, at twenty-one, at twenty-three, at thirty-seven. All those times I was in a place I felt trapped, useless, unworthy and a failure. Overwhelmed that I could not do what it would take to push through those moments, and I wanted to end that feeling so bad I considered the "unthinkable".

Unthinkable: *too unlikely or undesirable to be considered a possibility.*

The stigma and fear surrounding the word suicide, fear because it is assumed to be linked to extreme mental illness. This was a normal human response in a fight or flight situation with YOURSELF. This is the moment of feeling trapped with no way out, an overwhelming desire to escape the fear and pain that rises within. This is caused by triggers, failures, losses, shame, guilt, all low vibrational emotions and dwelling in them just feeds the beast. Another interesting fact I found was those who had not felt this way at some point in their life were the rare ones. These dark thoughts of wanting to leave this World have been widely programmed into our minds that any inclination towards this line of thinking is insanity. That is just not true. Everything has a way of working itself out and that is why you must work on loving and speaking life into oneself daily. This is why you need community if you do not have friends and loved ones to support you in your life. The true answer to prevention is the continued work on loving thyself and recognizing self-worth so that when these sledgehammers of life hit us, we have enough stored within to push through and rebuild. This is why a support group is essential in not only holding you accountable to love yourself, but they will push you in the right direction. In those dark moments, we cannot see clearly through the fog of suffering to understand we are being CONDITIONED for our next level. Life is not fair, never will be fair and you must navigate the storms on your way to paradise.

Just as an athlete must endure extreme conditions and fortitude to gain strength and perfect the skill to win...so must we in life. The next level of your abundance is not going to show up until your frequency signals to the Universe that you can handle that gift and not lose or destroy it.

We keep asking ourselves how we end up in these places in life? How is it I cannot seem to sustain abundance? When is it my turn?

There had to be a way to eradicate this impulsive and gripping thought of taking ~~one~~one's life. It ~~cant~~can't just be black and white like this. I couldn't keep going as I was and not have both a solution and an answer. I kept doing research and decided to go the esoteric route. The fear of the punishment and burning for eternity connected to taking one's life can be traced back very early Christianity. The impoverished people began to take their life rather than to suffer the hard life they found themselves in under that kind of rule. To prevent the people from making that choice, it became known by the church as one of the worst sins and deserving of the eternal fire. Because of a choice a child of God made under the harsh conditions of this life you will now face eternity of damnation. I do not think so. If God in all the perfection of creation and knowledge knew that creating an imperfect human would result in a great many wrong choices and mistakes, especially giving us free will. ~~So~~So, a beloved creation gets one shot at this? My God is a loving God every fiber of my suffering soul KNEW my son would be given a chance to change that ripple effect of suicide he left behind, beyond the grave, beyond what I understood yet innately knew. Somehow there had to be a way to change this trajectory and I had to be the one, I needed to find a way. I was shattered, broken, dead just not buried underground yet. I could not sit here and barely be a mother, no focus or even thought to a future self of vision for my family. I was drinking wine nightly, not sleeping, not caring about what I looked like, not even paying attention to my husband to see is he was OK. I was a statistic, a broken sad little mother whose kid took his ~~life~~life, and she never recovered. I could not continue this path because eventually I too would give into the desire to leave this World and cause this horrifying pain to occur to my remaining children, husband and friends once again. I would only make that ripple effect larger and stronger if I choose the same as my son.

Then who would stop it? Who would step up and find a way to eradicate this from my lineage, from my very soul? How was I going to do this?

"ENOUGH MOM, enough. Get up! Stop the pity party. How dare you give up when you still have the opportunity to breathe let alone LIVE. For every second you would have been with me you know need to find a way. Find a way to eradicate suicide from this family, from this World. GET UP MOM!"

It was my Jason I heard in my heart and mind that January 2013, almost two years after he had taken his life. There was no doubt it was him. There had been many other signs, and I wrote about them in my first book: OVERCOME, memoirs of a suicide. Yet that time, I took assessment of my life. I looked up from my fourth glass of wine as we watched the same show on the television after dinner. I glanced at my twins in that moment, now five, playing, giggling, happy? Yes, they had moved forward, young or not, they had found a way to have joy again. I then looked over at Brian, now sixteen, somehow functioning, not thriving but doing better then his mother. His brother, best friend and constant companion gone and the loss palatable, but he was healing. I then brought myself to turn all my attention towards my husband. He was thin, his skin had a gray pallor to it, dark circles under his eyes, exhausted. He had been carrying us all this time, working multiple jobs because I could not focus long enough to hold one down. He was doing the shopping for the food, cooking when I could not get out of bed, never ONCE complaining.

That wasn't the shocking part, what through me was that even with his obvious depleted state, he was looking at ME…like I was going to break.

GET UP MOM

So, I did, I chose to stop suffering and start finding a way to change the trajectory of this ~~families~~family's path. I chose to get up and so something. Broken in a billion pieces yet still able to glue some of those pieces back together. For my Jason, for my other sons, for my husband. I had to become unbreakable.

That was my first moment I realized while pain is inevitable in this life, suffering is a choice.

Chapter II
The Storm

There was an anger at the root of my finally getting up from my pity party that served me very well. 2013 I was determined to get us into a home and out of the crappy rentals that only one income could afford. We had a short sale just prior to Jason's death like most of the Country that has been hit by the housing debacle and after Jason we had filed for bankruptcy. Our youngest twin having autism and my obvious inability to focus made it very difficult for us to keep up with the bills and growing credit card debt with therapy and such. My husband always made sure the rent, utilities were paid, and food was on the table but how in the hell were we going to get into home ownership again. We did not have enough left over after each paycheck for saving. There was a very slight chance we could qualify for this new loan program and grant for those who had extenuating circumstances during their short sale, but the bankruptcy was not defined in those exceptions. The short sale came because I had four days a week of training to help my youngest son who had autism in our efforts to tach him to speak, go to the bathroom, speak, and just function, so that qualified. The bankruptcy came a year later, and obviously EXTREME circumstances and I felt we had a shot if I could find a lender willing to take a chance with us and be able to submit a package that the FHA guidelines would approve as indeed a extenuating circumstance loan. For two months I worked closely with a woman who walked that path with us. 1000 emails and countless documents showing everything from daily bank transactions to my son's death certificate because they needed to see the words "death by self-inflicted gunshot wound". March of 2013, I received the call, we were through the initial underwriting, and we could begin shopping for a home, we qualified! We had saved some tax return money to asst with the closing costs and granted down payment assistance from the state, all I had to do was find a realtor to represent us. We needed a realtor because it was going to be challenging convincing a seller this loan would close. While a few had received the initial underwritten approval, no one had succeeded in funding because final underwriting always found something that was not disclosed or that the circumstances really did not justify the outlined requirements to receive this special loan. Final underwriting does not occur until about 10 days before closing and the seller would have to list their home again. Most lenders attempting to get this type of loan did not dig deep enough to ensure the validity of the claim of extenuation and ability to repay and fulfill a new loan. Oh, but my lender and I had covered everything, and I had disclosed everything. I reached out to friends first who were licensed and because of our extreme trauma they were afraid to assist us because if the deal fell through, they felt we would be even more depressed, and they did not want to be a part of that. They told me over and over that it just was not going to close, there was no way that it could be done. So, I reached out to agents who assisted Fire Fighters as my husband was one and they would also contribute to help our closing costs. A first responder program that few agents were doing at the time. Yet when they learned of our extenuating circumstance loan approval, they walked away. Not one agent would work with us, no one. Not because they did not want us to get into a home again but because they just did not believe it could be done. They counseled us that even if we could find a seller who would take the chance, the loan would not close, and we had been through so much already they felt it would push us into a deeper depression. I had worked so hard only to have the door shut once again and I was angry! It was March 2013; two years had gone by in a horrible state of thick dark grief. I could not stay on this path. Every day I was sipping wine from lunch to bedtime. Every day I did my mom duties like a zombie, sometimes with silent tears running down my face. I would put my "mask" on long enough to go to small gatherings or friends' houses, long enough to keep the little charity for Jason going, but I was an empty fragile shell of a sad little mother. I remember sitting in my car because in order to have alone time I would go for a drive, sometimes for days. I sat in my car and just screamed like my skin was being torn from my body. The pain that racked my body having failed again and feeling trapped in a hell you would not wish on your worse enemy was excruciating.

Physical pain is one thing, your soul being slowly shredded into nothingness is a torcher that will forever alter your very DNA and have you question every last second of your existence trying to find tangible proof that YOU MATTER.

When I returned home my husband had gotten a hold of some medical marijuana and sat it in front of me. I stared at him, what in the hell was he thinking? Marijuana? I have not touched that stuff for 20 years and I am a mother!

"Why would you get this? How can I sit here and get stoned with kids and one with autism mind you!", I sternly said to him.
"Kimberly, you don't sleep, you drink every day, how is that good for the kids? How many times have you talked about killing yourself not being able to continue on? How many times have I talked you down from the edge? The anti-depressants did not work, and you need something!", he firmly declared

I have tried several different anti-depressants, anti-anxiety, therapies, nothing had worked and some of those pharmaceuticals had me holding a gun in my hand ready to go. They exasperated my already fragile condition. This was not something I was equipped to handle, and the normal venues people would go down to get that help had all failed.

"FINE!"

I grabbed the joint and took a few puffs. I did not feel much really, until I realized I was tired, that maybe I could lay down. Lay down I did and I slept more ~~then~~than two hours for the first time since before my son passed.

The next I woke up early and stood outside in the crisp air staring at the sky and picked up that join and took a few more puffs. This time it felt like someone had lifted a huge backpack full of boulders off my back and I could breathe. My face was wet with tears of relief. I COULD BREATHE AGAIN.

You can do this mom, you are smart, you always figure it out, find out how to get your license and YOU become an agent yourself.

It was him, my son, no question or hesitation, he was guiding me and I needed to quiet the whispers ~~in order to~~to hear him. That's what this medicine did for me, turned down the noise of shame, guilt, betrayal and suffering just enough for me to hear another frequency. I could hear my heart and there was no way my heart was ready to check out. She was mad as hell and ready to fight. The storm was ~~here~~here, and I needed to make my way through in order to give my family a new foundation, a new home, fresh energy and life so we could begin to finally heal. I walked inside, sat down at the computer still dark outside and began looking for real estate schools…nothing was going to stop me.

Chapter III
Thunder & Lighting

    I looked up the statues and laws to figure out how to write a contract and try and find some way to learn contract law. In doing so I stumbled across ads for real estate school, having bought and sold personal and investments prior to the housing bust, I knew the process just not familiar with all the contracts and process. While browsing, an ad for real estate school pop up on my screen. 90 hours, pass the school test and then the state test along with a contract law class and you were a licensed realtor in the State of Arizona. Back then you had to go in person and my husband's schedule as a fire fighter required 24-to-72-hour shifts. The only time I could go to class would be when he was home or my oldest son now 15 could watch the 5-year-olds. OK, I had found the time and now I need the funds. I pulled out our change jar and the tax return money and sat down and showed my husband that we had enough to pay the school fees and the licensing fees, all I had to do was get through the classes and pass the tests. He looked at the money and I realized he was confused because this was all we had for closing costs so if I spent it how would we cover the rest? The grant paid the down payment, but we still had a few grand in closing costs. I explained that we would still be able to cover the closing costs with my commission since I would be the buyer agent, and the title company would apply my commission right at closing.

I knew I could do it, I had nothing else to bring to the table right now. I had zero self-worth and zero self-love. Yet something inside me said TRY. He looked at me, knowing I had not gone past the 11th grade but was savvy as hell with a solutionist mind. When I applied myself in the past I achieved extraordinary things. I had been a millionaire on paper before the age of 30, yet I had also been through many life traumas even before losing my son. He looked at me, eyes filled with mirrored sorrow and said,

"If you think you can, I am with you, let's give it a try."
That's all I needed.

I sat down and studied the schedule; you could mix and match the classes, but they restricted you to three classes a day. I was in a hurry, we needed out of this dark cheap rental and into a new life. It was March and this month held both my birthday and the death date of my child. So why not make it the month of my new beginning as well. In eighteen days, I got through school and passed both the school test and state test the first time acquiring my real estate license March 31, 2013, not a day to spare and I met my deadline. At 41 years old, completely shattered and broker, I had focused my anger and did it. Forty-five days later, June 1, 2013, I turned the key to OUR home and watched as my young twins ran in, giggling and playing around in the natural light flooding in from the windows. My older boy picking out his room with excitement and planning how he was going to set up a little recording studio in his closet. The home needed work, clean but outdated and a project. I was grateful though to have found a seller who listened to me, heard our story and believed just as passionately as I did that it would go through. She took a risk and bet on me, and I made it happen. We had done it! The first extenuating circumstance loan in Arizona that closed after the housing bust by sheer will and determination that I could do it.
Yet that was not what shifted my trajectory on that day.
It was when I looked at my husband, standing in the kitchen looking out the window above the sink watching our twins play on the beautiful grass in the back yard. I walked over set the keys in his hand and closed his strong fingers around

them. Something changed in his eyes, his very essence shifted, and you could SEE he had his feet again for the first time since losing our Jason. In that second, I felt a tiny bubble of joy again. In that fleeting yet impactful few seconds I understood that purpose, service and achievement for others was how I was going to find life again.

~~So~~ So, at forty-one years of age, borrowing clothes from friends and hitting the pavement, I began to pursue a real estate career based on giving back.

I asked myself every day, "Kimberly, what do you have that these other agents don't? What makes you think you are going to succeed at this?"

The answer that came in then and still does today: YOUR TENACITY

Thus, was born Tenacious Real Estate and I became Kimberly "Tenacious T" Tocco, giving back up to 25% of my commission to help families and individuals who had been through hardships start a new chapter. I fought for them just as I fought for my family and having a past in corporate formations and negations, I was GOOD at it. I enjoyed legal language and quick thinking to find solutions and keep deals together. That first year I won rookie of the year, the next I doubled my sales and kept on that path over and over again proving the naysayers wrong. Brokers and agents would call me a "discount agent' trying to get clients by giving them money or that my idea of giving was not sustainable. In a way they were right. My clients were teachers, first responders, VA, special needs, military and by the time I gave them a portion of my commission and paid my broker and taxes, there was very little left. That did not stop me and by building volume I quickly became a six-figure earner, even having a six-figure month in March 2018. Seven years after my

Jason's passing and again in the month of March, fueled by loss and anger and needing put all that energy somewhere, I had achieved what some would have considered impossible.

I was driven by the passion to build a legacy for my son, to change that foundation of suicide and be able to tell our story and show that this had not broken me, had not broken the family. I had continued my private studies into trying to understand what had happened, why my son had made the choice he did and what that meant for his soul.

There is a deep ache within the heart of a parent who has lost a child that never goes away and having that "why" constantly echoing in my mind was tipping the scales on my sanity.

That year I had begun to hire coaches, went to empowerment meetings trying to grow and expand. Even though I was succeeding in business, I was still suffering with the loss and guilt and struggling with moments of suicidal thoughts. The typical "happy hours" that I had originally avoided started to become a frequent gathering. Masterminds and B2B became the way to collaborate and grow. I began attending some spiritual guidance sessions, both esoteric classes and philosophy along with the healing experiences and treatments. I still couldn't shake the guilt, so I stayed busy, distracted myself and aimed higher. I had been speaking out about suicide, sharing what I knew and experienced to possibly give more awareness and hope. I knew the only way I was going to reach people was by continuing to drive myself, people pay attention to successful people, and I just could not let go of the idea that sharing my story would make a difference. Not only was it cathartic, my story kept growing each time I pushed through and accomplished more. I was becoming a testimony of sorts, someone who had turned things around in her darkest times. I began working 50, 60, 70 hours a week in the pursuit of that success. It was the hustle decade it seemed, and I wanted to build a team and teach them this unique way of doing real estate. I took on new agents, cutting them in another 25% because I remember when no one had offered to help me, and no one can live off the 5% other teams were offering. The standards in the real estate community were to only give new agents a small cut and they had to pull in their own leads to get more, or they got nothing. Something about the idea of taking them under my wing and feeding them it would be reciprocated. Little did I know. I was giving back to my clients and my agents, selling large volume of homes but only bringing in 50% of what was normal for other agents. I taught myself how to edit videos and creatively directed unusual listing videos and started my own podcast. Big names loved my story, wanted to work with me or have me at the meetings but they also wanted to change me. I was different in that I wasn't looking to fit in but blaze a new trail. Yet also very insecure, still full of doubt so I began to lean into my ego more and I had a side of me that was "not so nice". I leaned into the masculine energy a woman who wants to succeed in a man's world does. I did not like how most handled their recruitment and real estate referrals. I had to learn the hard way that most people look at the money first and the people latter. The more money that was made, the more shenanigans went on behind the scenes. I started to gain attention, and I allowed that to go to my head, this is what happens when you get lured in by opulence and adulation.

I had died that day holding my son, that death lingered for a long time silently. I had achieved something since that time, I was revitalized, feeling successful, attractive and special. I stopped focusing so much on the purpose and turned to financial freedom, accolades and material gain. I was no longer listening to the song in my heart, but a vision influenced by those I surrounded myself with.

I had a hard time navigating the underbelly of the real estate community and it started to pull me in. It was manipulative and everything was based on your volume and who you were rubbing shoulders with. Certain players who had big names dictated a lot of what happened in the industry. It was almost like a mini-Hollywood scene, a lot of drinking, parties and people sleeping with each other regardless of marital status. I had no interest in being with another man, especially after what my husband had survived, but I enjoyed the attention and being flirted with. I felt something other than the drive to succeed, I felt desired and that is important for a woman. I would stay later at the events, mingle and get to know everyone I could. It was good to be known as that helped when presenting offers. Recognize the professional and know they will work hard for the deal. Gives you an edge. As I had begun to make a name and a brand for myself, I became infatuated with the game. I went to as many as I could, broker opens, charity shows, podcasts, masterminds, I loved both serving and the accolades. Winning multiple awards for philanthropy, inspiration, overcoming and giving back. I was thinking this is how I make it to the top, play the game they want you to play but try and do it better.

None of that is true of course, for the most part that is. The best way to become known in this industry is being ethical, true to your word and obsessively on top of things so the transaction is seamless. Make yourself valuable with skill and knowledge and meditate on the vision of who you want to become. Carve a niche out for yourself that fits your authenticity and uniqueness. Attract to you the people that your energy works best with by embodying the vision of what you want to create as an entrepreneur.

I caught the attention of HGTV for one episode of a new show they wanted to launch in Scottsdale Arizona called POOL HUNTERS. There are no coincidences, I knew if I was truly going to truly write the story of my son, I would have to become successful and "known" for it to make a mark. I had a list of goals to fit that requirement and HGTV was on that list. Part of what I became known for was my unique listing and recruitment videos. As I did not have a marketing budget in the beginning I self-taught myself how to edit and in my youth, I had been in commercials and print so I used my story telling abilities and created attention grabbing videos.

I always said to myself and later taught, if you are going to produce something to showcase who you are, use the best of your abilities and budget to not just throw together an "ad"; you sit down and make it a Superbowl Commercial!

Those videos along with my new podcast caught the attention of the casting director and I nailed the qualifications and conditions and found myself filming the inaugural episode.

**I had set aside my promise to Jason that I would write our story, publish the book and launch the second phase of our light train. The day I got to see him after they had prepared him and set him the coffin, I had asked to be with him alone for a while. They had done a beautiful job, I could see where the bullet hole was, centered on his forehead but they patched it very well. I looked at every eyelash, the curve of his perfect

nose, the slight curl to his forever short hair. I sat there over an hour just looking at him when my husband came in. The entire group had come for the rosary blessing which we did the night before his funeral. I looked at my son and said out loud, "I won't let them forget you, I won't let go son. I will be better for your brothers, I promise. I love you my Jason, I love you." I asked them to close the lid, I did not want any of them to look upon my son this way, they had done a wonderful job, but I did not want anyone to remember my son like this. They would remember his glorious green eyes and huge smile; they would remember his laugh and his generosity. THEY WOULD REMEMBER BECAUSE I WAS GOING TO TELL HIS STORY

I went back to writing, I had an outline, and it was time to lay it down, time to use my gifts. Writing had always been my most loved creative outlet. Through the studies of the metaphysical I understand the alchemy of the written word. Truth laid down on paper becomes the testimony for the broken heart of another. This is why AI will never be able to replace the human who is tapped into thy higher self and allows their very life force to spill upon the paper. My son was going to get all of what I could ~~give~~ give, and it was going to be glorious.

"There is nothing to writing. All you do is sit down and bleed." – Earnest Hemmingway

By the time the inaugural episode aired in July of 2019 I was halfway through the writing and up for a huge award with my brokerage. That is when the jealousy and haters began to enter my life. The sponsor I was under at the brokerage started to show his hidden side, controlling and narcistic. He began insisting he could interview people just as well as I was doing and if I wanted to see my productions grow, I needed to work on creating HIS podcast. He also spoke about writing his book and not even acknowledging or showing enthusiasm for any of my work. These were also fully recorded in studio productions that I was editing at home in between running my real estate business, events, training agents, and filing and editing my own podcast. I was receiving more attention, and people truly enjoyed the content and the different ideas on giving back or building a business on gratitude. He didn't like not being center of attention thus way he made the request that I assist him start a podcast, do more videos for his side health company, and at the time I truly believed that he was doing this to assist me and advance my career. No offer of compensation, no names going under my down line but definitely pushing me to 70 plus hours per week. I was thin, not sleeping well and those old thoughts of worthlessness were coming up again. I saw all the red flags but chose to ignore them because he had such a big name in this business, there is no way he wasn't what he said he was. I had brought the owner of a huge team to the table and asked my sponsor to set up a meeting so we could bring him to the company. An addition like that would change my family's life bringing thousands more per month in the company compensation plan. A few weeks later he called me at 8 in the morning, I will never forget, I was driving on the 51 freeway, and he was excited telling me he had fantastic news. I felt a shift as he said that, not in a good way, he kept going on about how he makes his best deals while sitting on the toilet in the morning and he just did it again. I found that really odd to say but I kept listening to him go on and on.

"…so you know, you understand a guy at this level, well he isn't going to join under just anyone and especially a woman. Lots of people going after him trying to get him to join, offering packages. I offered him 10,000 shares and of course everything that we ~~dod~~o, and he said yes. But just to be clear, he is joining under me, like I said, he was not going to just come over under anyone."

I felt sick, I needed to pull over. Did he just say what I think he said? Did he ~~actually take~~take my lead and negotiate with him privately without me and take him as his own acquisition?

"~~So~~So, look, this is great ~~news~~news, and I will make it up to you. We will get others, come on this is great!"

That was the year prior and now here I was, buried even deeper under the haze of misogyny I had refused to identify back then. When was I going to learn my lesson and how am I supposed to move on now that I have built all of this with him and this brokerage? It was when I went to launch my book, the planning began January 2020, he and I now butting heads often the months prior and things had just gotten worse. I was drained, still not getting paid for all the efforts on his videos and podcasts, still no agents in my downline as promised, not spending any time with my family just working continuously. I called to express to him I just couldn't do it, I needed some agents to help bring in leads as I was still the only one with leads. I needed him to start paying me for the production work because I was at a point of breaking and struggling myself with suicidal thoughts again. He had no empathy for the mental struggle I was having and insisted I get over it and find the time. He had been giving the studio some money for the room time and incidentals, but I was not getting paid for the hours of work involved. Videos and productions like this were getting three to five thousand an episode and I was doing them for nothing. I had produced his first full episode, filmed three more and launched the second one when he called to tell me I had stolen his joy. Tenacious Productions was fully producing, directing and editing these episodes and all those hats were worn by me. I had committed to launching every Thursday and when I tried to reach him for the launch he had been socializing at a party. Therefore, I launched the episode and several hours later I had gotten a call from an inebriated, jealous man. I had taken his joy because he wanted to write the description, and he did not want anyone to see my name affiliated with it. He continued to say that because I launched it from my account everyone could see it was me that posted it.

This man wanted everyone to believe that he had done all the work, he wanted the accolades, he wanted my expertise yet had no intention of honoring that service. After an hour of his explaining how I stole his joy and it was very late, I hung up the phone. Early the next morning he called demanding I take the video down, which of course I did. The conversation turned into a match of wills, each trying to prove points and that is when he pulled the superior card. Began lecturing me on how to heal my soul and that I had work to do. He was not wrong on the work that still needed to be done but how dare he try and tell me about healing from the things that I had already.

"Until you have had a child commit suicide and…", I had started to say in reply to him.

"WHAT! WHAT DID YOU JUST SAY TO ME? YOU JUST CURSED MY CHILD! WHAT IS WRONG WITH YOU!" he spat into the phone.

"You did not let me finish, until you have had a child commit suicide, and you have been able to recover from watching your child die, that is when you can lecture me on healing the soul."

He was no longer listening, screaming now on speaker phone with his wife in the room that I had cursed their children with the phrase, "Until you have had a child commit suicide." He had completely lost it, in a manic tirade that was quickly turning violent. I suddenly woke up sitting there, at least enough to realize I had put myself in this position. I had felt it all along but choose to ignore all the red flags.

I had chosen this personality type my entire life, the manipulative narcissist, because I still had not healed from the childhood trauma of my mother. We tend to draw the same people to us until we learn the lesson and recognize what we need to heal.

After an hour of his continued screaming over the phone my husband took the phone from me and even then, it took several minutes for him to realize he was no longer taking to me. My husband confronted him with the way he had been speaking to me and that this conversation was over. He was in a rage and called out my husband asking him to meet him because he was going to take him down. He kept repeating this is how it works, his way, his process, this is how he deals with people who can't following instructions and had insulted and cursed his family. Of course, my husband being trained in terrorist negotiations was calm cool and collected and agreed to a conversation meeting for which the tyrant never showed. I had seen the same thing happen to other agents and assumed like many others that it was the fault of the agent not the high-power co-owner who was an "inspiration." So many things were now clear but that did not stop the feeling of worthlessness that I felt. Waisted time, I had wasted ~~to~~too much time and effort going AGAINST my own intuition and allowing the ego to dictate how my story should go. I had joined forces with someone who had no intention of seeing me rise to a level that drown him out. I had been week and sank back into old programming instead of believing I could make my mark all on my own. Like I had originally intended, my unique vision for my OWN path. I had to go back to the quiet and listen to the song in my heart, back to journaling, my routine, back to find me. I had a book to launch and people I needed to reach with these words, this story, and the stories of others. I was going to take my podcast show to the stage and produce stories of overcoming inviting a few guests on stage who had faced impossible situations and made it through. I knew that people just needed the tangle, needed to actually see hear and FEEL the energy that comes from being in a room of broken-hearted humans who finally have hope again…who have curiosity again. It was time to ignite that within them again, the zest for what comes next, the "God Spark" as I began to call it.

I severed the connection. I recognized my part and mistakes and walked away. Gave up what I had built with the brokerage but not what I had built for me. Solo agent once again but free and feeling excited for the launch of my now completed first book. I was curious to see if I could do it, I had something I felt would be a great success in spreading awareness. <u>OVERCOME: Memoirs of a Suicide</u> finally launched nine years to the very month of Jason's passing. March again, only by now that month of sorrow marked a month of greatness. I had learned to do something magnificent to transmute the suffering of that month. I never knew how I was going to be emotionally, so making sure I set goals and planned a joyous occasion was key. My continued studies with the esoteric and metaphysical had begun to calibrate in my mind and a deeper understanding steeped in.

The journey through the many different aspects of what has been documented about the afterlife in all cultures, religions and beliefs is daunting. It does not always click or even make sense, many times I would read something or take a class and feel both elevated and confused. But it was coming together, and I could distinguish certain areas where I had control over my gifts. The more I opened up in my exploration of the esoteric, the sacred geometry and patterns of the Universe, the clearer the understanding became. What was once foggy and sounded like babble became the window to everlasting "life". I had learned enough of the language of the spiritual that I could now read and more importantly…comprehend.

March 11, 2020, my 48th birthday, the book I promised him I would write made its debut and it was going to be a magical experience. The book was a raw, in your face truth of what we faced that day and the most important moments of those years following. It was a testimony, cathartic, writing out all the insane thoughts I was having, purging unto the pages. Walking the reader through the raw ugly truth and explaining what I did to push through. Each word I wrote I purposefully envisioned healing. That whoever were to read the pages, they would come through the journey shifted. I had tried parent groups, suicide circles, therapy groups and all I felt and heard was sorrow and comparing stories and it never changed. Just sitting in the story. Never moving forward from it, like when the parent never changes the child's room. Stuck in stagnancy and that is suffering. The ugly of the story, the parts we never want to share, the reality of how dark it got and what you had to do to crawl out of that hole. Just as my podcast interviewed stories of overcoming, I brought 3 stories besides mine to the stage of a packed room, and it was GLORIOUS. My vision was to launch the book and show and then start speaking all over locally and eventually, nationally. Speaking on stages was not as much of a commodity prior to covid. This was going to be my "Safe Haven" events, breaking the silence of suicide and marking a safe place to hear the "ugly" of the story. A new way to bring prevention and awareness that we all have struggles, we all suffer. It was a huge success, and I had never felt so sure of what and where I was going. We were already talking about the next one and people wanting to sponsor before the night was over. I felt my son the entire evening, he was proud, and I was on fire!

March 13, 2020, just two days later, covid hit and that dream went with it.

Chapter IV
The Sun broke through the Clouds

FIRST CHANNELLED MESSAGE IN 2020

March 13, 2020 4:06pm
I was overwhelmed by the need to write down this message in my head. I had been sitting at my desk and grabbed a legal pad and a pencil. I had never felt something so clear and so strong come through. There was no question of divinity in that moment. I felt the spark of oneness, I felt the God Spark. I began to write quickly because it was already fading.

Families are forced to stay at home
Cleanse the Earth of Darkness
Bring them into love
We are the Leaders
This is your Kingdom
This is why you feel the need to travel
You are being called to lead the Chaos with love
Only those who feel the calling of love will make it through this decade
Religions and Governments will be reconstructed
The leaders who will inherit the Earth are the ones chosen by the People
The people will choose the ones who love them---and who loved them first

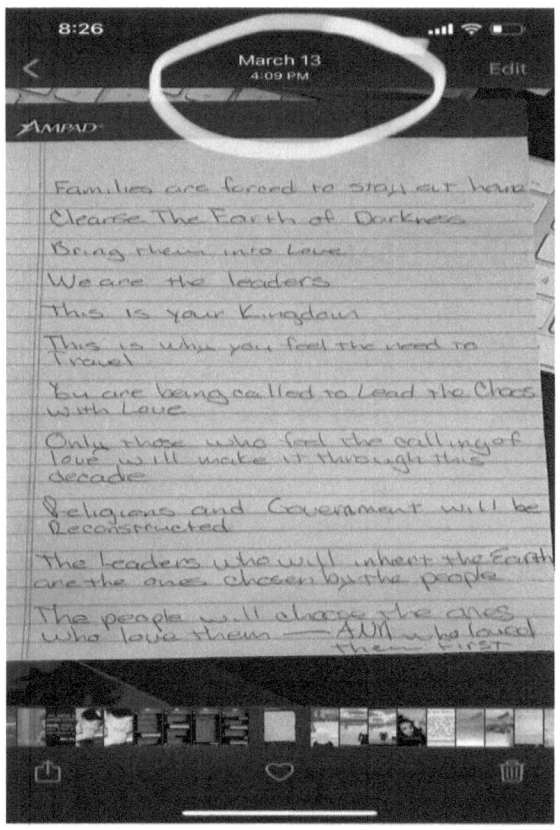

As quickly as it came, it was gone. I felt high in a way, like when you are sitting outside on a bench in the park, grass is green, and the breeze brushes your cheek. That kind of high. Like the rest of the World, the next three month we were under lockdown and isolation. I sold our last rental property and built my dream pool and sanctuary in my back yard. If this was going to be our final days, then I was going out laying on the Baja pool shelf of my lemurian paradise. Meanwhile I let go of the dream, I let go of the hustle, I just accepted that the shit had hit the fan and here we go.

After a few months of the chaos, we all began to see the charade and I had been studying as much as I could about viruses and origins, CRISPR and such because it just felt so orchestrated. In the interim, one of my spiritual teachers invited me to study with some of her other students at the incredible Delphi Metaphysical University in Georgia. I was still doing real estate, but I had burn out. The last several years had really put me through the wash and the shutdown, in all honesty, could not have come at a better time. February 12, ~~2024~~2021, I stepped foot unto the ancient Cherokee grounds South of the Blue Ridge Mountains, the grounds of Delphi Metaphysical University and my entire world went into turbulence both extremely profound and soul healing, yet also the facing of every dark corner you have chosen to hide from.

The language of God is silence
In order to hear God you must quiet the noise
To quiet the noise, you must find the silence
To find the silence means facing what makes the noise
To face the noise, you must accept that it occurred
To accept that it occurred you must step out of emotion and observe
To observe means you are standing in the silence, and nothing can hurt you here

I found the silence at Delphi and cracked open a huge vault of unseen trauma and yesterday's stories that I was still holding onto down deep inside. ~~In order for~~For your gifts to become stronger you must purge out conflicting thoughts and energies within. A fitness enthusiast purges out sugars, carbs and toxins to get his body in prime function and physique. There are generations of trapped trauma energy. This is the process of epigenetics, where the readability, or expression, of genes is modified without changing the DNA code itself. Tiny chemical tags are added to or removed from our DNA in response to changes in the environment in which we are living. These tags turn genes on or off, offering a way of adapting to changing conditions without inflicting a more permanent shift in our genomes. This is passed in the lineage and if you understand the possibility of past or linear lifetimes, then you also understand the depth at which these traumas have built up. So as you chip away at the layers of ~~built up~~built-up trickster energy, you will need to go through things, periods of what is called "Dark night of the soul". They were not far off when they spoke of a MATRIX, like the levels of a video game, you must keep trying and discovering the secrets of that level so you can move onto the next. During the course of the game, you receive rewards, additional life and weapons.

These gifts are our weapons, your ~~life lines~~lifelines, your power up to arm yourself and take on the next challenge. You unlock both new and power up the ones you already are working with each time you push through. The prize as you push through and persevere? The euphoria of KNOWING and no longer flailing around wondering what the meaning of life is. The silence has answered those question and now you practice mastering that knowing. Here are the basic gifts of the esoteric World.

Clairvoyance
Clear seeing: The ability to see or have visions: to "see" things presented to them within the mind's eye. We see these mental flashes which include pictures of people, scenes, places, objects, spirit, symbols and colors.

Clairaudience
Clear Hearing: The ability to "hear" messages. Messages are being transmitted directly into your mind. At times you may

hear a non- descript voice, music, or even radio like conversations

Clairempathy

Sensing emotion: Everyone can sense emotion but Emphatics sense or feel emotions from individuals lingering energies of others. The ability to access other people's emotions and can sense their happiness, joy, elation, pride, sadness, anger and fear. They can also take on this energy very easily, so this path is not for the weak.

Clairsentience

Sensing feeling: This is the classic 'gut feeling' or intuition. The ability to sense and feel emotions from beyond the flesh both positive and negative. These feelings are being transmitted by your higher self, sometimes others or angels and are clearly different from your own feelings. You can receive warnings this way as in feeling that something is not right or get an excited, elated feeling when something wonderful is about to happen.

Clairalience

Sense of smell: When a certain fragrance or odor that is being transmitted by telepathic reception. Like walking into a room and you smell pizza or pipe tobacco for someone who smoked or the person's favorite perfume. Also flashes of memory or vision when a scent triggers deja'vu.

Clairgustance

Sense of taste: You can "taste" essences being transmitted by beyond. Souls, energy can transfer a character or behavior influence to us and sometimes it comes in the form of a flavor. This is usually something that they loved while they were in body.

Clairtangency

Touch or feeling: This is also known as Psychometry. You are able to receive a message by touching or holding an object in your hands. The object is personal and has the vibration of the owner in the composition or material of the item.

There is truth in the power of a collective coming together in belief for a singular cause and to connect to that SINGLULAR, you must fine tune those gifts. That is what Delphi did only on steroids. I was ripe for knowledge, I was seasoned in being a victim, martyr, hero, savior, I was ready to just…be…me.

That first week of studies cracked open so many layers that for the first time ever in my life, I finally felt truly calm. The hum that sits just beneath the surface, the one that holds the whispers, it was ~~quiet~~quiet, and I could feel peace. I had no intension of seeking certifications in any of these fields, I was only going to this session_s~~ ~~because I felt so disconnected without vision of where I was going to go now with my business. This was 2021 and it was time to get back to focusing on my future as that was what kept me from sinking back into that lost sad little mother. Distracting myself with work and success had kept me away from facing the true "caged one" within. Delphi shifted me into a complete other realm where the possibility of magic could once again enter my life. Losing my son had obviously done a great many things to my existence, but the one thing I had accepted is that I would never again have that magic, the alchemy of passion for life shattered with is last breathe. That kind of magic, the will to live in greatness on epic levels.

…because ~~its~~it's not enough to just live, you must want to choose life

Oh, but now I had the understanding, I could answer part of the "why" questions that festered in my gut when it came to his choice. I could see my path once again and how I was going to pivot and continue what I started. Metaphysical real estate, the first of its kind was next on my list. I had already been working with energy, counseling my clients, doing masterminds, panels and guidance sessions along with the gift of being a house whisperer. I was extremely good at transmuting and reading the energy of a home down to what it will sell for or what it can be acquired for. My business had been going long enough to have solid numbers to reflect the success. Tenacious Real Estate would now have a certified Metaphysician and Spiritual Psychologist. I could still speak on zooms and venues which would then serve all aspects of what I do. Fit foundation, fit body, fit mind, fit soul. These were just a few of the things that came out of that first initial visit where they teach you how to deep channel. I also had the opportunity to receive healing sessions from some of the master's which I found to be crucial in the sustainability of that peace we all are needing. As I spent my last afternoon on the grounds, I mapped out the classes and special trips back for my own personal healing. It was going to take almost two years, but it was exactly what I needed. My business was doing ok, but I was so unhappy with what I had not achieved, thinking of the daunting task of rebuilding a team. I had expected myself to have become hugely successful by now, yet here I was starting over yet this time I had years of training and experience with hundreds of clients. That was the short cut. If you can find a way to compact the knowledge of decades into days, then you cut your building phase to almost nil. My twins were teens and barely paid attention to us any longer, as is the way of a teen. My husband and I had drifted further and further apart the more I dove into my metaphysical studies, attending events and wanting to keep striving for my dream of traveling the World and meeting group who needed what I was bringing. A new frequency in prevention and self-awareness. A different look or take on mental illness and the choice of suffering. I wanted to eradicate suicide, and I truly believe it's through good old fashion storytelling and sharing because I understood frequency and a voice has healing power. Not just listening to someone's voice but the alchemy of purging out your own sorrow to be heard. The exchange of truth then lifts that darkness and transmutes, resets the cell. Then the experience

of that healing propels you into wanting to share and listen again, thus the ripple effect. Each story, each share, each listened too are the prescription for stepping away from suffering, finding community and self-forgiveness.
I digress
I knew what my next phase was, I had just finished the graduation ceremony on the grounds of Delphi and was walking back to the main building in drizzling rain. It had been cloudy all day but the euphoric feeling of knowing was coursing through my veins. I had such a shroud of divine covering about me, I knew who I was in that sublime time. As I walked along the path thinking all these plans through and feeling the excitement in my belly, there was a sound of thunder and the clouds suddenly broke open. I looked up but it was ~~to~~too bright on my eyes after that full day of drizzle and gray. I quickly grabbed my phone and took a picture. Just in time as the clouds closed back and I say I was standing at the top of the outdoor staircase down the ~~the~~ kitchen hall. A student stood at the bottom of the stairs looking up past me with her mouth open.

"Did you hear that?" I asked her inquiring about the thunder
"Did you see that!" She explained!

I walked to the bottom and stood under the porch to look at the picture, I instantly started to cry. Some people see one thing, others see something else, yet all see divinity. I will let you decide on your own.

*My second book, <u>Tenacious Angels</u>, details the incredible journey of turning my soul inside out and the discovery of self-love and self-worth

This was my tangible, the proof that I needed to know I had not lost my mind. This was my sun that broke through the clouds. If this is ~~crazy~~<u>crazy,</u> then there is no place I would rather be.

Chapter V
Turbulence

I would travel to the University several times, yet it was the second visit, the study of advanced channeling that the prophetic vision this book started with occurred.

June 2021

Delphi Metaphysical University ~ 2nd visit and course in Advanced Channeling

This will be the coming of a New Era to blanket the Earth for the Universe is feminine and she is calling back her voice, calling back her blood. Look for the dragons, look for the feathers.

Do not lose faith little one, stop playing small, embrace who you are, embrace your light, walk in your regal self, let go of the things that distract. We will care for you; we will be with you and help you. It's OK to show the World without saying anything of who you truly are. Your gifts are ready to emerge, you must open the door and call unto you the Great One who will support you and this path. You are whom you always believed and it's not that you are better than others, you have KNOWLEDGE that needs to be shared. Take the time to learn and develop and be selfish for you have gifts unto which the World will benefit only if you ALLOW yourself to come into you. STOP PLAYING SMALL

This journey is for the own self. Speak for you and no one else. There is nothing you need. The memories are of the lessons learned. Like a child now off on her own, you must fly the coop. Spread your wings, nothing else matters if you just take care of you, listen, voice, write and what comes of that creates a vibration that has not been here upon the Earth as of yet. Orion was lost because you used all your energy and wisdom to try and fix everyone else. Fix YOU and others will naturally follow. Walk YOUR truth and all will be revealed. You do not need to fixate on being a leader and saving the World. We only need you to save yourself. The point of all of this is to show you that you only need to care for yourself this time. Naturally you will through the works of healing thyself. Elijah spoke and he asks that you step each step as the Queen you are, the sophisticated, beautiful ancient knowledge of who you are. The ripple effect of this will affect the past present and future. For Jason yes, but all others for whom are deeply connected. Stay calm, stay focused, observe, be pensive, have joy yes but do not give in to "small" of the past and hold the position of who you are. It is not arrogant; it is taking your place amongst the Kings. To love and be a servant of knowledge and peace. LEAD WITH THE LEADERS FOR IT IS THOSE LEADING IN LOVE WHO WILL BE CHOSEN BY THE PEOPLE FOR THE PEOPLE.

I felt during this time of learning and trying to evolve my business that things would become easier, like the delusion everyone teaches you about manifesting. There are "gurus" who will tell you that all you must do is think about it so much that it appears but what many forget is the physical work involved. While the law of attraction certainly requires that deep strong emotion of conviction, you still need to create the vision! As you elevate you will also face more difficult challenges and forces that will distract and stall you. Questioning everything you did and why you started this in the first place. This is why it is a practice, there is a process and levels to this existence that is much more complicated than having a happy dance and wishing for a million dollars. We have evolved enough to understand energy and its flow. The rituals and practices of yesteryear are exactly that, yesterday's magic verses today's true alchemy.

Magic is typically understood as the practice of using supernatural forces to manipulate reality. Alchemy, on the other hand, is an ancient philosophical and proto-scientific tradition that originated in antiquity.

This is a time of revolution, of reset and the beginnings of the paradise that was intended from the start. Heaven and Hell are not outside oneself or the Earth. Being human IS the portal of entry. We decide our destiny and we make this existence heaven or hell by our choices, actions and thought. We are given this gift of having a human experience to create what our soul could only conceptualize.

You must practice the vision daily, fine tuning it, burn it into the memory cells

You must engage in the activities it will entail to become that version of your self

You must discipline the mind, body and soul and prepare for the battle so the vision can live

You will be knocked down to test your resilience

You will break in order to test your expansion

You will want to give up and give in almost as much as you want to succeed

You have the gifts and the talent to create the vision

You have the strength and the courage to push through and see it done

You have the resilience and the tenacity to keep moving forward

But you cannot do it alone and that is what the vision from the mediation was telling me. We were shifting into a new era that historically takes place when humans leap in evolutionary advancement. Technology, AI, the slow programming and desensitization of our society has left our humanity expendable, and most are not going outside, building community in person or going a day without being attached to their phone. The loss of the symbiotic connection to the Earth, to Gaia, the mother that truly provides for us. History shows genocide of the indigenous people in every era and rule. Divide and concur, pillage and destroy pouring all those lives of the innocent into the ground and then building foundations for them to continue the reign of fear. Desecrate and rip away the ancestral knowledge and traditions that balanced the planet calling it evil and of the devil when all along they were darkness slowly spreading through all our DNA. We have separated ourselves so completely from the natural nutrients, environments, the voices and song of our true past that we have completely forgotten who we truly are. Instead, we have replaced our gatherings of honor for bars and football games. Celebration no longer holds deep reverence and gratitude for days together, it's a quick hour once a week of words spoken for performance not transcendence. our body needs and replaces it with artificial light, artificial synthetic foods and even artificial AI friends. In the beginning, we were created to exchange energy with the planet, as we intake the food of the land we also are the fertilizer to the soil. Our bodies were capable of long life, repair and rejuvenation. Our bodies are made up of minerals all of which are found in the Earth. Greed, opulence, power, control separated us from true balance not to mention religion and spiritual beliefs. This is why we are feeling as if we are in the "end times", we are so far off balance on all levels that we are indeed heading into a great reset.

From 2020 through to September I would fly back to Delphi and advance both my healing and degree, my business started to pick back up, but I felt so alone.

People often feel utterly alone during the process of both overcoming suffering and trauma and trying to get to know that person in the mirror again. It can lead to a profound shift in perception and understanding, causing one to feel disconnected from those who do not share or understand their experiences. As you release the trauma within, face it and work on creating a more balanced and clam you, that self-discovery can be isolating. Peeling back the layers strips away the security of belonging. If you do not recognize the person in the mirror, you have lost your home so finding that group or place to lean into is essential.

By September I was well on my way in working through those dark whispers and I could look at myself in the mirror and know I have a home; home is where the heart is. I went back to writing and created content and videos that let out my passions that gave me joy. I developed the platform for being the Country's first certified metaphysical real estate agent and was ready to launch. I had taken assessment of my accomplishments since losing my son. I had reached a six-figure income with real estate within 2 years and held steady, launched my podcast, made it on HGTV, spoke in many groups, podcasts and stages and my first published memoir hit number one. It wasn't enough, I still had a fire for sharing stories on stage and bringing more awareness and healing. I was capable of so much more yet could not advance past this stagnancy.

It wasn't enough

I should have millions by now, I should have expanded my business and reach much further by now. In order to make the dream happen I needed to generate the monies that it would take to fund the events. I was exhausted again, still struggling with keeping my marriage together we were both so different now. We had been through so much together, but the magic seemed gone. Gone with my son, gone with the woman I used to be. I had to be thankful that I found something still burning within that demanded I honor my promise to build that legacy. By chance, which nothing is a coincidence, a friend sent me a flyer about a speaking contest called, *The Great American Speak Off*. I had never heard of the ~~host~~host, but I recognized the logo, 10X. The contest was ~~similar to~~like American Idol only for speakers. It stated there was going to be open auditions in five days! I signed up and started to do research about speaking contests and who Pete Vargas and Grant Cardone was. I had recognized him from the show he did many years ago but had not kept up with him. I felt confident this was exactly where I needed to be, my story is something I had been sharing and speaking for years. I arrived early to the venue October 15, 2022, the lines were long but again, I felt confident, I looked and felt great, and I was ready. I registered and checked in then was told the first audition round we would be given sixty seconds to speak.

SIXTY SECONDS!

How was I possibly going to tell my story in sixty seconds? I watched and listened to other contestants. All I had to do was deliver the shocking truth of what happened to me that started me on this path. Go straight into the day I lost my son, quote the statistics and who I was.

I made it through the first round! Now to do it again.

Second round clear!

That top 150 were then given 2 minutes to speak and all I did was expand in details and a bit more of my why hoping it would be enough. As we gathered back in the auditorium, on the screen they brought up the winners of Golden Tickets who would be headed to Miami for the Semi-finals. My name was there...

I was very emotional, thanking my son for guiding me and proud of myself that I had made it through. A chance to finally get in front of a ~~world wide~~worldwide audience, both as a contestant on the pilot showing of the contest, but to be in front of thousands at the finals. My gut told me I was going to make it to the top three, I saw the vision and I wasn't letting go of it. However, this experience also showed me I needed to get some training. Much had changed in the speaking World since the lockdown, and it had become more of a self-pitch of services and business then it was just inspirational speaking. There was a formula now, speaking was basically a verbal resume of who you are, present the problem, the emotional connection, the solution and offer your service. It was a savvy business model because everyone has a story. Knowing that people love to talk about themselves and turning that into both a competition and training to use the story to make money, brilliant. I realized I was in over my head and remembered from many of my past mentors and business coaches, you ~~have to~~must pay to play. Pay I did because I WANTED this, needed this because I no longer had that curiosity to even push myself any longer. I felt deep in my soul this was going to be our moment, my son and I.

I went home with the golden ticket and shared it with my family. The now teenage twins did the typical nod of the head and mumble under the breath a simple congrats. My husband was happy for me but not at all excited about the competition. When I told him the cost of the classes and coaching, the look of disappointment nearly broke me. No one was really excited about the "public figure" side of my business. They didn't like the camera or attention so it's difficult for them to understand why I want to pursue this because they have never attended an event or a large charitable fund raiser.

"I ~~have to~~must do this, I know I will win, I feel it and its exactly what I need to start impacting others on a grander scale. I will make it pay for itself with booking more healing and guidance sessions. Please understand and don't be disappointed.", I passionately explained to him

"You have been speaking out and working and building for years and now you want to build again? Why isn't this enough?", he inquired.

On many occasions I had asked him what he used to dream of becoming when he was a kid. Every time he would look at me and say, "All I ever wanted was to be a husband and take care of my family."

"Because this is what I have to do, I have felt this dream of impacting not only others but truly making a difference, to be remembered because then they remember Jason."

He sat for a minute looking at me, I could see his face soften.

"Please make this the last time, I worry about the impact if you should not win. If you don't win, then promise you will realize you have achieved enough and now we can just plan for our future and work on our retirement."

I was thrilled he was on board but no there were conditions. He had stood by and allowed me to follow my intuition for a long time, he was signaling he needed a quiet life now. I could not blame him, he had never stopped, not once to grieve or take leave to heal. He had put his head down and provided for his family. Double time, second jobs, cooking, shopping, he just wanted his family to be OK and he buried himself in that duty. There was no question where his priorities were focused; he was a man that dedicated himself to the well-being of his those he loved. A good man. He was right though, I was tired, I had been going at this since literally two days after Jason passed. It started with wrist bands, then the small baseball charity, interviews, real estate, all of it because I didn't want people to forget my child. I needed to make his death mean something other than a boy who walked upstairs and shot himself.

Humanity's greatest philanthropic movements have been born from her deepest sorrows.

My sorrow was deep, and I was going to rip it from inside my broken heart and hold it up for the World to see. I was also going to show how my broken heart remains unbreakable. No amount of turbulence could deter me from my course in that moment.
…in that moment, I was ready for the storm.

Chapter VI
Here comes the Storm

December 12, 2022

Packing for Miami, I cannot find my wedding ring. I find myself in a panic mode, $20,000 custom made ring with special blessings for my children said over it and I can't find it anywhere.

It triggered me.

I sat on the floor in my bathroom, everything weighed on what was about to transpire over this next three days. I had taken the lessons, prepared my speeches, worked out daily, woke early, I had done everything right. But the whispers of doubt had crept in, I felt so alone in this process. I realized I had felt alone for a very long time, even prior to Jason. Thoughts of taking my life flooded into my mind, old programming when I started to feel the disappointment in myself for having lost such a precious ring. I knew how to handle it now, I sat on the floor of my bathroom and aloud myself to cry, aloud myself to scream and then sat quietly. I put on my ear buds and began to play modern classical and stood up to wash my face. I looked in the mirror wishing for so many different things all at one time, racing thoughts all over the place.

"Look at me."

I spoke this out loud to myself and looked straight into the eyes looking back at me.

"I love you, breathe, you look incredible, this is a distraction. The ring can be replaced, this opportunity cannot."

This is how we transmute that energy; the one frequency fear is afraid of is love. Love thyself, shake it off, keep moving forward. I turned from the mirror and fished packing, ready for my 3:30am alarm to catch an early morning flight. I had never been to Miami and was truly looking forward to this experience. I had a lot of anxiety, but I was able to channel that into excitement. I had arrived a day early to prepare and adjust to the time difference. Fresh sharp mind for the competition. I had planned my clothes changes because we had to prepare to change two times if you advanced so they could make it look like the next day when truly it was filmed at once. I had decided to wear one of my most graceful gowns in deep royal blue. The contrast of an elegant woman who could pass as a pageant Queen speaking about the suicide of her child was memorable. There were one hundred and fifty contestants there from across the country. There had been thousands of auditions and here I was, with the top semi-finalist. That did feel good, and I was confident, feeling beautiful and powerful. We had five different room to go into with a different scenario in each. Four rooms we had sixty seconds and one room two minutes. Each had a judge and cameras backgrounds, lights, etc. The first room I went into had us speaking to the camera as if we were doing a live zoom. During the speech a large light tipped over, but I just kept going, no flinching. Turns out that was the test, they purposefully set it up to trip you up. I aced it, the judge shook my hand and said, "Great job, you didn't even flinch."

This is how the day went, I did well in every room, I spoke to many of the contestants, encouraged others, learned from others, I did what I loved to do. I did have some moments that I felt I could have done better of course, but I was proud. I FELT it, I was going to make it through. We broke for the night as the next day they would be calling the top thirty then down to the top twelve who would go in front of the superstar guest judges. From there the judges would pick three to speak at the 2023 10X Growth Con. That was the stage I saw myself on. I needed to get in front of those judges, I knew that if I could just get in front of them my entire future would change. It was a knowing, there was no mistake, whoever those judges were, one of them would see me.

The following morning, I rose early as usual, enjoyed a long bath and dressed in my second outfit bring a spare 3rd if I made it to the end. Today I went in my signature jeans, boots and a silk top. Lots of jewelry today as I was feeling sassy and maybe even a bit conceited, I was proud of myself. We all gathered into the room to hear the call of winners, Grant Cardone came in to announce and it occurred to me that he and his wife would most likely be judges, I wonder who else it would be? Like American Idol and America's Got Talent, this show would have judges giving instant feedback, but the audience would be the ones to decide the winner. The audience for this episode would be those of us who did not make the final list of thirty and then twelve. The twelve would perform on stage as we participated as audience members This being the pilot show, they had not sold outside tickets so really needed us to stay.

Stormy Wellington

That named popped into my head as Grant continued to talk about the history of how this competition came about. Stormy Wellington was a woman Pete Vargas continued to talk about all through the first auditions, through the trainings and beyond. He would say she is one of his favorite speakers. I had become curious to see who she was just a couple weeks prior to coming to Miami. Pete Vargas being the genius behind this entire 10X Stages production, I wanted to find out. I looked her up on instant gram and saw she had a live going so clicked on it. It was early in the morning, so she was in her robe and brushing her teeth, brushing ~~he~~her teeth! I loved it, she did not give a rat's ass who was watching, she was sitting there speaking her truth and living her life. I clicked on her profile, 1.4 million followers. I watched a few reels, she was sassy, dressed loud and sexy, spoke without apology. I loved her.

She is one of the judges

That's how it works sometimes, your intuition, psychic abilities, whatever you want to call it, you hear it, see it, feel it. I went to my phone and looked up where she resided, MIAMI! They began to announce the top thirty, name after name, it got down to the last name…and it wasn't mine.
I sat there, at first it didn't register, how can that be? All the signs, everything pointed to getting in front of the judges and I have been cut. Over the announcement they were reminding us to stay as participants and to be good sports. Some people were in tears, others angry and left the building. I do not know how many minutes went ~~by~~by, but Pete Vargas came out and said that he decided that one person he had seen did not make the cut and he felt this person deserved a chance. This had to be me! Once ~~again~~again, the name was called and once again it was not me. The name called had almost walked out and they used this as an example of why we should stay, you never knew when there would be another chance. We were to be back in two hours as they took the thirty contestants down to twelve. I kept my composure, walked out to the rental car and sat in there and questioned everything. I guess this was the sign that I was done, I needed to let go of the dream, I had promised my family, I had to accept it. I had asked for an opportunity, I was given it, and somewhere along the way I just didn't cut it. I felt this deep hole inside, that part of me that would never be whole again, failure. I had committed to the show, I needed to clean off my face and

make my way back to the auditorium and stick out the remainder of the day.

Smile on, looking fresh, I sat in the front row, if I did not make it to the stage I would at least be animated and give it my all in cheering on these that did. I certainly was not going to allow my ~~ego~~ego, and my disappointment control the rest of this day. I had made some good ~~connections~~connections, and I was determined to enjoy this moment. Pete Vargas then brought out the judges, he was one of the four, Elena and Grant Cardone another two, and then out came Stormy Wellington. The voice I had heard in my head was accurate yet what good did that do me now? I was just here in the audience, no way I could present or even meet her now. True to her image I had seen on Instagram, she was dressed so fly. Sexy, sassy and wealthy with a huge smile on her face, you could tell she was in full control. The stage was ~~set~~set, and the judges took their seat. As each of the final twelve came out and the judges gave their feedback, it was Stormy's voice and her words that rang authentic and true. There was also something about the cadence, the tone, her frequency could be felt to the bone. Her advice was nurturing, yet stern, she also was very funny. Out of the four, her presence dominated without her even trying. I noticed a very large bodyguard not far from her at all times which had me curious. It was more ~~then~~than just being wealthy; he was there to protect her not just from being robbed. As they wrapped up the show, the stage had the winners, judges and some family members shaking hands and getting ready to leave. I wanted to meet Stormy, I truly had no interest in meeting the Cardone's, it was Ms Wellington that I knew I was supposed to connect with. They finally allowed us to come up to the stage to shake hands with the judges as they began to walk off, good thing I sat in the front row, I made a b-line for Stormy. She was reaching down to grab people's hands as she walked off and

I caught her hand. She looked straight into my eyes, and I immediately heard:

FIRST LEADER

Just as quickly as her hand and eyes met mine, she moved onto the next and the moment was gone, but not the *knowing*. She was the one from my vision and I was going to study her and try to understand this strange turn of events. I had to go home and face the music so to speak and submit to the promise I had made. The pursuit and dream of making it big so I could build this fantasy legacy for my son had reached its end. I would continue the real estate, helping families who had been through hardships start a new chapter. My twins were fifteen, my oldest twenty-six and it was time for me to settle at fifty years old to the second half of this life. I could continue to expand my knowledge; maybe even finish the second book I had begun. I had set it aside thinking this would be my grand finale' and ending to book two, winning a spot to the finals and major exposure. Now what? I felt so empty, so alone, so misunderstood even to myself. How could I possibly have gone from the peaks of success just two years before to this empty shell of a woman? All the work in healing, all the schools, teachers, meetings, events, coaches, books, for what?

I was to exhausted and disappointed to stay on this line of thinking and I knew how to pull myself out of these horrid dark clouds when they come in.

"Do not stumble over what is behind you, leave the items in the rear-view mirror there and keep your eyes on the road. Breathe, watch a movie on the plane and let it go for now Kimberly.", standing in the mirror of the hotel ready to leave for the airport, I spoke words of truth to myself. Acceptance is key in moving forward from anything. We must accept that it occurred and there is always a reason and a direction your soul is pursing on your behalf. This does not negate free will and the traumas and events that will occur, but it allows us to understand flow. Change comes when you are in so much pain from your suffering that you finally choose to step in another direction and let go. As I waited for take-off, I came across a few of Stormy Wellington's YouTube interviews and videos. I clicked on one from the 10X Growth Con in 2020. She was dressed in another one-of-a-kind outfit that just had me excited to see a woman this success and confident yet free with her personality. As I watched and she began her talk, the explosive energy and impact she had on the thousands in the room and anyone watching on screen was unforgettable. How could someone watching not realize that this woman was greatness? From her truly terrifying childhood to how she made and maintains her multi-million-dollar businesses, she was impressive as hell.

She was speaking about energy
How to speak life into oneself and overcome
Manifest your vision
She was an alchemist
She was powerful

I clicked on her site and like many leaders in the network marketing and speaking fields, she had many different offerings, but I was looking specifically for something she spoke about in that video, her community called Girl Hold My Hand. Yet, why bother? I had made a promise, I set my phone down and settled into the long flight home.

Back to reality…

Chapter VII
Hurricane

Once I settled in at home, I prepared myself for the holidays and the year ahead in this new position, the position of giving up. I took assessment, as I once did that fateful day in January of 2013 and looked at everything I had achieved, everything that I had lost, everything that I gave up on. Man, I had done so much! Considering where I came from, what I had to carry on my shoulders, I had done well, maybe that should have felt good? The real estate sales now bringing me to what they call a "million-dollar producer" meaning, I had made over a million in commissions, HGTV, launched and reached #1 in my book sales, started my podcast with both video and audio on all channels. On paper it looked amazing, but it wasn't enough. I had given a lot of that commission back in rebates and helping other agents, made mistakes on investing in the wrong programs and coaches, and also blew through it enjoying life with big vacations and spoiling myself and family. I was never one to just do "well", I wanted to leave greatness behind when I finished this pursuit of legacy. I realized as I learned the metaphysical understanding of the soul that I was no longer doing this for Jason, this was for me, and no longer for the outside accolades. I needed to make a mark and that fact that no matter how hard or how much I had pushed myself I always seemed to come up short within my own expectations. That made no difference at this point because I no longer had the answers. I had gone as far as I could go alone and finding the right mentor had been challenging to say the least. The motivation and drive was gone, burned out, I was exhausted.

Stormy Wellington

That push again, why was my thoughts continuing to drift back to her? I went to the Girl Hold My Hand site and signed up for the monthly private community. It was mostly zoom being that they had global members, and the headquarters were in Miami. Within a few days I received a call from Sheila Woodward, someone I assumed was from the organization. She introduced herself and began an easy conversation asking about my goals and why I had joined. I was actually excited to have received the call, took me off guard truth be told. I was used to calls from these types of companies, yet Sheila did not come across as a sales agent. She was the real thing, a woman of success, caring and compassionate. She listened to me, heard my story and reflected value on all that I had done with authenticity. She wasn't looking to boost my ego or self-worth just to see why I had joined the community. She called to genuinely get to know me and encourage me to see myself. She brought up an event Stormy would be speaking at and that she was trying to get a large group of the community there.

"I don't sell tickets, I sell visions.", Sheila explained as I inquired about the event, she was encouraging me to attend.
I remembered what it was like being in the same room with her and the vision from 18 months before in Delphi
"I have not heard someone speak like her before in person. I have been to so many events, had so many coaches and mentors, let me just start attending these morning meditations and zoom calls and see how it feels. When did you say they start?"
"8am, Monday through Thursday, hop on the call.", she replied
"Oh well, I have my own morning routine, I cannot say I will be at every one of them, but yes it sounds intriguing." I cautiously replied

I was one who had risen at 5am every single morning as part of my healing and sustainability. Knowing how to transmute trauma from the mitochondria, the deep organelle in the cells, I would rise before the sun, no phone or alarm, light a candle, get a cup of coffee and play with my dogs as the sun came up.

The study and discovery of the morning sun having a profound effect on one's balance and calm helped me develop this routine. When you have experienced extreme trauma, be it mental of physical, the memory cells of the brain and mind have been altered. Neurochemical, structure, long term stress impact on the physical body. It's an open bleeding wound that can only be repaired with calm, peace and silencing the suffering. By training the body to wake gently, no alarm (use songbirds if you need something to wake you) no blue screen phone, no bright lights. I wake, light a candle, make a cup of coffee or tea and sit outside with my dogs and wait for the sun to greet me listening to the symphony of birds singing the praises of waking another day. First light impacts the circadian rhythm, enhances mood, increases energy and vitamin D, and creates discipline necessary to sustain healing.

I would journal, pull my tarot cards, and this allowed my body to gently wake, easing the automatic response of anxiety PTSD ignites within. I did not want to mess with that and 8am east coast time meant 5am my time, I would have to see how things went first.

"Listen, coach has not attracted someone like you, let's stay in contact, you want to be in the room Kim. Send me your book, I will see if there is an opportunity to present it to coach.", Sheila encouraged me.

I could do that; I could give it a shot and it was indeed exciting thinking that maybe Stormy may read my book. The following Monday I did just that. Woke a bit earlier so I could get my coffee and sat outside as the birds began to sing and hopped onto the Zoom call. The first face I saw was this cute little gal about my age, giggling and struggling a bit to get the sound on zoom right and make the morning announcements. She felt somewhat new at this, but you could see she was doing her best to hold down her nervousness and open the call. I scrolled the attendees and as she continued with the announcements those numbers kept going up and up, hundreds attended this mediation! Impressive but I had seen huge influencers and millionaires have clubs and memberships of this size so that might be a reflection of her long-time presence and members. *I wonder what they will be doing for the meditation part. I doubt we will see Stormy Wellington herself*, I thought to myself. At this level the owners just did not have the time, nor did they want to spend time on simple calls that were not money producing. That's why they are millionaires, their time is very valuable, and their team aligns them with only money-making activities.

Just then I heard her voice and that beautiful face, no make-up, in her pajamas and clapping her hands telling everyone

HAPPY MONDAY EVERYONE CAN I GET SOME FIRE IN THE CHAT!

Wait now, hold up, wait just a minute here…Miss Wellington is on this thing? She is just waking up and on this call? I sat there hanging on every word, she was sharing some issues she was going through, sharing successes from the weekend, she was speaking to this group as if we were all at her house having some coffee with her. It was a completely different side of her and one that I could connect and relate too. Her social media presence captures a lot, when she went live the authenticity and her personality really came out but this, she was completely relaxed and giving us her all. She then took us through her ten-minute meditation, and we all signed off by saying, "Today is my day!" I sat there for about an hour just reflecting, going over everything from the speak off to what I had just watched and took part in. There was no question I needed to stick around and find out what was meant for me in all of this. I adjusted my morning routine and as I closed out 2022, I was a full participant in the Girl Hold My Hand community. I ordered on of her books, *The Quiet Storm* when I learned they were doing a live read on the book on the Instagram platform. She had launched several books, but this one was about her beginnings, and I wanted to know why she was different, what she had gone through for her to understand suffering the way she did. It was rare for me to see that kind of understanding in someone's eyes when it came to the strength it needed to become someone through the hurricane of sledgehammers that life delivers. Find out I did, at many points reading the novel I would set the book down and try to comprehend the choices she had to make in the most terrifying of situations a CHILD should have to face. From her conception, her mom's almost aborting her, foster care, avoiding molestations, her brother shot in the head and running into the shower still alive needing help, to stripping at thirteen to get food and power, first baby at fifteen, the sledgehammers just kept coming at her over and over again. I adored her, she found a way, she discovered her purpose, and she went from high-school, baby momma, stripper foster child to a multi-millionaire and the World's most successful black woman network marketer and public speaker. Making over fifty million dollars in eight years and more importantly, coaching hundreds of others into millionaire status. People who had given up, homeless, suicidal, single mom's, families who had been through hardships. This is why she started the community, because she didn't have anyone or a group to support her, not through childhood nor through her efforts to change her life. She stepped up and chose to scream to the entire Universe:

"I WILL NEVER BE BROKE ANOTHER DAY IN MY LIFE."

I called Sheila and had put my deposit down to attend the Break the Code event organized by Alex Morton, another ~~big name~~big-name speaker I had yet to see in person. Stormy was a keynote speaker and Sheila was right, I needed to get into the room, but this was more than I had ever paid to "be in the room". If I was going to do this it was going diamond level because I wanted a chance to learn directly from Miss Wellington and hopefully, make an impression. Stormy did things differently though, we were not just going to watch our coach present, we were going to walk in and make our presence known. Sixty of the Girl Hold My Hand members were also going, and they were making custom jackets for us to wear so there would be no mistake who we were here with. I was a part of something that was not just business, not a club, this was a truly connected family of people who were at all different levels in their life and businesses.
…but I did not tell my family

I knew they would not understand, I knew they would be disappointed. I had promised to give up on the dream, stop spending money on marketing, education, events and just settle into the mother and wife roll who did real estate. While my real estate business was steady, I had gone into debt trying to make this vision of fit foundation, fit body, fit mind, and fit soul come to fruition. The Metaphysical Real Estate and Spiritual Psychology went well to together because most of my clients had been through hardships not to mention being able to honor any religion, beliefs or traditions to enhance the experience.

The feeling of that fateful day when I handed the key to my husband and I could see he had his feet again, that always lingered in the back of my mind when working with clients, friends and family. I wanted my clients to have that feeling, that shift into a better tomorrow.

"Why can't this be enough? What are trying to achieve? You are so good at real estate.", my husband was confused, he just shook his head.

We needed to save to get ahead, but I want to succeed so that I could do it all! I could not bring myself to settle when a new chapter had opened. There was nothing more he could say as I had already made up my mind. There was a part of him that recognized the importance of me having a strong passion in something I was trying to accomplish. He knew without that; I would sink slowly back to that dark place that almost swallowed me whole.

The key is to be curious enough about the next five minutes that you want to stick around and see what happens. This is the first thing I teach my clients in spiritual psychology, always be curious, even when life has ripped out your heart and stamped on it. Don't give up, wait for the opportunity to rebuild and expand its capacity. The heart has memory cells very similar to the brain, scientifically proven by *Dr. J. Andrew Armour*. ~~In order for~~For the capacity of expanded storage we must first break out the encrypted data, the trauma memory cells. Then we put it back together and search for more pieces along the way to becoming who we are underneath the crust of programming and trauma this life has put on us. Some call it karma, others say pay back. We are meant to live a life of enlightenment yet in order to step onto that path we will need to break through the lessons of the past and that is a painful experience. There is no avoiding it, you must face ~~all of~~ all your fears and trickster energy so that you can pull it up and transmute it into life giving energy.

I was staring at my fear, guilt for choosing me again, and holding my breath. All of this had to mean something! I could feel that hum just below the surface, *keep going.*

The early mediations fit into my routine, and I watched, listened, learned. Stormy shared her moments of challenge, failures, wins, plans, spiritual channel, all of it. She was a leader, that was not the question, what became obvious was that she was anointed, here for this time. I knew what was happening to our Country, to the planet and the entire system was on the verge of collapse. My prophetic channel March 13, 2020, the leaders will be the ones leading in love and the ones who loved the people first. Miss Wellington loved the monies, but not above the people. She was the people and the people were her.

It doesn't matter where you are in life
You can speak life over your life
I remember the day that I didn't know where I was going
What I was doing
I remember having to speak life into myself
I didn't wait for a profit
I didn't wait for a pastor to speak life over my life
I will motivate my own self
As a matter a fact, I will speak these very words:

I AM DETERMINED, DINAMIC, PERSISTANT, AMBITIOUS AND FAITHFUL
A BEAUTIFUL, SOFISTICATED PROFESSIONAL, CALLED TO BE A LOVING, WORLD RENOUNED MOTIVATOR

~~I AM DETERMINED, DINAMIC, PERSISTANT AMBITIOUS AND FAITHFUL~~
~~A BEAUTIUFL, SOPHISTICATED, PROFESSIONAL CALLED TO BE A LOVING, WORLD RENOUNED MOTIVATOR~~

MY NAME IS STORMY WELLIGNTON

These are the things she would teach us, speak life unto oneself. She would bring special guests to some of the zoom meetings, people who would share their story and success. This felt like home to me, sisters I needed as my family had all passed but my remaining children and husband. I had not been excited like this, not even after winning the golden ticket, this felt right. I was also very unsure of myself, not of my knowledge and skill, unsure I would fit in long term. I was different, not just in style and personality, but in the way I process and work. I was travelling to Miami to attend the Break the Code event, purchased Diamond level so I could get to the dinners and gatherings at Coach Stormy's home because that was going to be the best way to speak with her. A multi-millionaire with over 1.5 million followers isn't readily available for conversation, everyone wants to present and speck to these elite professionals thinking they will get the break they need. Unfortunately, this puts the successful professionals on the exclusive and elusive because everyone wants a piece of what they have built off their blood, sweat and tears. I understood this very well having been around this level of wealth in some of the masterminds and coaches I had previously. I took the time to watch many of her older videos, finished reading her book and felt I had a good understanding and truly just wanted to learn and possibly get some opportunities to pick her brain as they say. On the flight over, I watched *WOMAN KING*, a 2022 historical action-drama film about the Agojie, an all-female military unit that protected the West African Kingdom of Dahomey in the 1800. Watching this movie re-confirmed I was indeed on the right path, Stormy Wellington is a Woman King, and she was going to be one of the great leaders showing others how to free themselves of this controlling system, of things.

When you have opened the mind to the possibilities of more, you begin to see and understand that society has restricted the learning by labeling other ideas as blasphemy and heresy. This is not to say that certain religions and beliefs are wrong, but the specific instruction to stay away from any teachings other than that one is a control agenda. If the word of the teachings is truth, then why would that change by reading another book or studying the ancient principles of Universe? By stepping into metaphysical studies to better understand the soul and purpose of our existence. I also opened up a treasure chest of information and studies throughout history that showed me a broader version of God's plan, or the plan of the Creator. As this knowledge is understood, so is the divine connection to intuition and visions. There are many individuals who are quoted in the bible as having visions; Daniel, Ezekiel, John, Joseph, Moses, Isaiah, Ananias,

Mother Mary and Yeshua all had visions and premonitions. It is not because certain people are chosen by God, we are ALL chosen. The more we come to understanding that the gifts of the esoteric are our inheritance, the more balance we will find amongst each other. Each one and all of us has access to what lies beyond the vail. This is what the great leaders, spiritual guides, profits, tried to teach. We are all part of the great IAM, tiny droplets if you will of the conciseness of the creator. The more I studied, the more answers I found, the deeper my calm and peace bloomed within my broken heart. To want your neighbor to thrive, to serve the agenda of healing the polluted dying planet, to feed hungry children, that is paradise. Not your Hermes bag, the club membership, position in societal adulation or the number of cars in your garage. Success is how many lives you can impact and change not how many shinny objects you can collect and show off. The only thing you take with you is who you become and who you become is who you shall begin in the next transition… ~~Yet,~~ Yet I digress.

The event and watching her speak, meeting all the women who came to be a part of this movement, I had never experienced that before, EVER. Stormy had the idea to make sure our ticket prices included the custom make Girl Hold My Hand Jackets so that we could show unity at this event. As I was obviously beginning to understand, this was unlike any group I had been a part of. This brought you back to your mother's house or that home, safe place you had as a child. Even if you had a rough childhood, we all had that one place or relative that when we were with them, we could sleep, eat and relax because the love was tangible. Girl Hold My Hand is TANGIBLE because its real and that is what love is. Like any other group people become active with, you form quick bonds and Sheila Woodward along with a handful of other gals quickly became my sisters. Again, something I was not use to, most women in business were competitive and even if they showed a pleasant exterior, behind your back it was never for your benefit. Not this community, not these women. They had grace, compassion, kindness and the wanting to build together. When we were at the event, all of us wore our matching jackets and sat together making the bond and energy between us even more powerful and Stormy would come out and speak directly with us as "her girls". The last day of the event she decided to have the Diamond Elite level come to her personal home and enjoy the beautiful resort back yard, break bread together and enjoy the friends she brought to speak with us and uplift us. Elena Cardone and Gary Breaka were amongst them and as the night wore down, I had a chance to sit with her and speak.

I wasn't ready for her; I opened my mouth, and nothing came out. I felt completely inadequate and unprepared. *UNWORTHY*, was the whisper that went through my mind. I had failed on so many levels trying to reach the top, I was forgetting how truly talented and successful I was. Instead, I made small talk, shared a few thoughts and my opportunity was gone as she moved along trying to give all of us a chance to present and speak with her. The next day as I packed and made ready to fly home, that thick dark cloud of disappointment began to come over me. I had spent all this money, invested even more money in systems and processes that I thought I needed only to find myself in no better position business wise because what good does all this do without the knowledge or leverage to use it? I had spent my real estate commissions that I should have used to get ahead of debt and did not have the courage to ~~really even~~even speak with her. At the airport I broke down and had a beer, then two, and on my connecting flight I missed it all together not paying attention to the time. The suicidal tendencies rose up in my throat like bile and trying to hold it back was like walking on coals.

You IDIOT
How stupid are you
Pathetic little nothing
Old, ugly, worthless

I tried to get on another flight but there were no more departing that evening, so I was going to have to sleep in the airport, fortunately there was a hotel inside the terminal but that was more money that didn't need to be spent. I called my family, my husband was kind and spoke to me gently, he knew I was on the edge of darkness. He had seen and heard me in this state many times, one of the reasons he wanted me to stop pursuing this dream of mine was knowing what it did to me when I didn't reach my goals. I found the hotel, got switched to the first flight the next morning and sat in my room thinking how much better everyone would be without me here.

That's what happens when the fog of suicidal thoughts float in and take over, sinking you down into that dark place. You feel like a cancer that should be cut out from this World. For some, it is a failed relationship, the ripping out of the heart and slamming it down on the ground for it to be stomped on. For others, it's the stress of not being able to provide for your family, not knowing where the next dollar is going to come from. For me, it was the inability to stabilize my trajectory and unify it with my vision for myself. The allusive dream, reaching it just long enough to touch it, only to have it slip through my fingers and start all over. It was not so much me that I could not face, it was my family, all those who had relied on me, had success with me and continued to grow from the encouragement. How is it I could help others achieve but here I was, sitting in a hotel room in some airport a complete mess and ready to just die? That's when the phone rang, an old friend from a long-failed relationship, the one human on the planet that could lift me from this space. The one and only person who knew me better then myself and he spoke to me for hours pulling me back, giving me freedom to express what no one but him would understand. Everyone needs that one person they can share their "ugly" with. As the sun rose, I was ready to get on the plane, I had a plan together, I was going to fight again. I still had a chance to make this work I just needed to stay focused.

Suicide is a permanent solution to a temporary problem and without a community or person to talk you down off the ledge what do you do? This is the problem I needed to solve, for myself first and foremost and then from there, develop a module to give others the same. To many times I had found myself in this place and I could not shake that trauma energy of suicide and knowing it was always going to be there, I needed tools to battle the impulse. So many losing their life to the real pandemic that has spread across the planet, the suffering and weigh of it slowly taking over our every thought. The resources available are great, 988 to call if you are in a bad state, online groups and different techniques if you learn them like face tapping. Yet having been in that space many times, those were the last things on my mind in that moment. A seed needed to be planted within the memory cells of the mind and heart. A spark that would ignite during the time it was most needed. The idea was something I had started to form a year before, this episode of almost taking my life once again enforced the need.

Once home I hid most of the issues and went back to the daily meditations at 5am. Observe, learn, listen, keep pushing. Over the next several months I applied the techniques Stormy showed us, I became a useful member of the community because I wanted to serve and show gratitude, and selfishly it gave me joy. Even if I was on the edge, I knew I had these women, I knew they would be there every morning without fail. Coach shared deep thoughts and emotional moments with us, her struggles with people that would take advantage of her, business partners who betrayed her, or just flat out left. I came to understand that I was truly not alone in this struggle, here was one of the most powerful women in the Country and even she was fighting off the crap that life tended to throw our way. I was a lot like ~~her~~her, and she was a lot like us, just a different level of wealth and resilience but same problems.

To understand what she had faced as a child and how she persevered, threw everything she had into making a difference and making money. She was "unfuckwithable", touchable but you could not stop her. PERIOD

She is what I needed, the voice that put me straight. I was back to writing, selling real estate and in line to clear six figures again. The next opportunity to spend time with her was going to be at the 10X Growth con in March and I was not going to miss it. I was giving myself the best investment, I was fortifying my foundation for choosing life. Once again, we dawned our Girl Hold My Hand pink jackets and dozens of us all sat together in Las Vegas while we watched the finals of the Great American Speak Off for which Miss Wellington was the judge. This was the final and as I sat there wearing the pink jacket, I could not help but feel how ironic it all was. This was where I thought I would be, but on stage and not watching the finals. Yet I WAS there, and I had sisters now, I had family beyond my own children and husband. By now I knew through her teachings that everything that is meant for you will not pass you by and sometimes the things that pass us by are not meant for us. Earn your way, serve your way, pay your way, and I was doing all three because when I followed her guidance, I felt aligned and balanced.

The sledgehammers would come but I had a foundation filled with others that held me up. My hand was held, and I was holding on right back. Sheila Woodward had also become a mentor, I made sure to show up on time, not late and extended any assistance or guidance I could to others. It was at this event I would begin to understand the emergence of the deeper meaning behind this draw to serve in this community. During a break, Sheila and I had been watching our section of seats to make sure we had them saved as our community group here in unity together. I saw a woman not art of the group and looked at Sheila and said,
"~~Hey~~Hey, no worries I will walk over and kindly explain why we are holding these seats."
Sheila gently grabbed my arm and said,
"~~No~~" No Kim, you cannot do that."
I stood there for a minute and looked at her, back to the woman now taking a seat, and back at her.
"Kim, you are a wonderful person, but you are new here. We earn our place through integrity in this community, loyalty to coach and the well-being of her community. You need to earn that authority over time and service. Pay attention, observe and grow. I will go have a friendly conversation with her." And with that she gracefully walked over and charmed her way as she does. Sheila Woodward a force to be reconned with.

She was a gorgeous woman, petite with skin like butter and the most perfect face. This woman knew how to get her monies, from radio personality and station celebrity to fashion designer, interior design, high end jewelry sales, fitness coach and much more. There was not a place that Sheila went that did not see a huge increase in their sales. She is the woman with the magic touch. Sheila had been with Miss Wellington for years, was a founding member of GHMH and worked tirelessly in service of both Stormy and the members as a volunteer! She was not on anyone's pay roll. At one point, Sheila was calling and checking in on thousands of members, mentoring, encouraging and helping the members see their VISION. She was also responsible for 95% of all event tickets sales for coach. Sheila would call until she sold out the events with record breaking sales numbers into the eight figures. She earned her position and yes, she does take home commission from those sales as she should. She doesn't sell tickets, she sells visions. Just another testimony on how many opportunities become available when you plant the seed.

By the time Stormy had her Awakening Event in September of 2023, I had launched my second book, *TENACIOUS ANGELS*, the deep journey into my own soul and finding answers within. I had not been able to finish it because of what had happened with losing the speak off and almost taking my life in January. I had lost the creative energy needed to put my all into the writing. I had to ground myself and find my feet again and that would not have happened if Stormy Wellington had not crossed my path. I did not miss a morning, I did not miss a weekend, I stayed consistent with all that the community had to offer, so my life stayed consistent. I had even auditioned for another season of the speak off and tried out for more. I did not make it through but at least I was trying, and I had booked several podcasts and small groups, I was getting the word out about eradicating suicide. What your think about with deep emotion, you bring about. Stormy would shower us with these golden nuggets of wisdom daily and it kept me on par with my goals. More importantly, we aligned in the drive to want a better life and her energy was pure abundance.

I also got to witness her diving deeper into her divine feminine, her calling to be that in which I had seen in my premonition. She always had spoken spiritually not dedicated to any religion yet knowing the word of God, she knew scripture. She had read books like *Think and Grow Rich, The Alchemist* and she often read us quotes from the Ma'at, the book of the ancient Egyptian laws of the Universe. She had even gone back to Nigeria that summer where the Yoruba people were of her lineage, her family. Further confirmation for me that she was the *first leaders* from my vision because the Yoruba people are the original alchemist, metaphysical magicians; the field of study that I am also certified in. Coach often spoke about honoring your ancestry and bloodline, especially your mother. She had lost her mom, held her mother's hand as she took her last breath August 26, 2011. Another synchronicity between her and I. I lost my Jason in 2011, taking his last breath in my arms. Her mother had been a drug dealer and went to prison several times as she was growing up and unfortunately that left Stormy in foster care and horrible situations. That did not stop her from loving and honoring her mother. She had pictures of her everywhere and held the Awakening Events on her mother's birthday. So many areas of my life had lined up with what Stormy had proven to be able to overcome. My father had been to prison twice and left us with my mother was deeply disturbed, and we grew up in an insane household that could be wonderful one day and the next she was beating the crap out of you and making you go without food to teach you a lesson. She was extremely narcistic and had borderline personality disorder and when my father got out of prison the second time, he was a broken man and became a drunk. Stormy's example helped me find the path to forgiveness for my mom, something that had festered in my gut for a very long time. The first day of the awakening she spoke of her mother, and I felt the well of tears fall, I could feel forgiveness in my heart for her. Stormy was expanding and in person, it was palatable. The way she brought in the drums, the timing of the guest speakers, the artistry in her vision of each day let alone the POWER as she channeled her message on stage. She never memorizes her ~~speeches,~~speeches; she allows God or spirit to flow through her~~-~~. ~~Of course~~Of course, she has a topic and ~~outline~~outline, but she free speaks, without script, it comes directly from the heart.

LEADING IN LOVE

The final day of the event was approaching, the day on her yacht with those who went diamond elite. I was ready this time, ready to have my face to face and really present to her who I was and why I was there. I dressed in one of her personal kaftan's bought from her daughter's boutique because I felt like a queen when I wore it and I felt WORTHY.

WASHING OF THE FEET

I had been receiving confirmation after confirmation that I was on the right path, my work was improving, the calm within was more prevalent and steadier. I had made a few more bad investments, but those failures only went to fortify my resolve to stick with this woman. As you grow in the speaking industry you must be warry of the traps as well. I began to understand that you must invest in your systems, training and businesses to grow, you can only take yourself so far before needing that advisor or guide. I was paying into masterminds, marketing retreats, speaking camps, tens of thousands of dollars only to discover I was the sucker. Some of the masterminds were well worth it but the marketing and speaking "gurus" are a dime a dozen and Stormy Wellington was the most powerful woman speaker in the World. What was I thinking not investing all that money directly into what she could teach me. I walked down to the ship feeling so free, we all gathered and waited for coach to arrive. I picked a seat right in the center and when she came on board, I listened and made sure I took the opportunity to speak and interact. It was a small group of only twelve of us, Annetta Powell was there another extremely successful woman who had been to prison and now lived the life of a multi-millionaire. REAL people who wanted to share their secrets and interact and help you reach your goals. You get one shot in this type of room, and you take it when the opportunity presents itself. Three times I was able to "present" myself and ideas and one of those I opened up to her and expressed how I did not feel worthy the first time I met her.

"In order for a person to truly spend this kind of investment to learn up-close and personal with you like this, they have to feel worthy of it. I did not feel worthy the first time I had the opportunity to speak with you. I needed to get to a place that I did feel worthy and this last nine month in this community brought me to that place, you brought me to this place."

She was not surprised by this, but she was impressed to my admittance of it. She knew it, she had felt this many times and for her to hear it from another admitting it was confirmation. She truly appreciated my expression, and it felt good to be myself and seen. The weather was turning, and I began to look around to see if we had time for me to present the story of the washing of the feet. I knew it had to be on a ship because that was the vision I had. Not only the past life vision, but this one. In my vision, there was a circle of people, women on the deck area of a large ship, Stormy was sitting, and I was explaining what the ceremony meant. I went and got bowls for a couple of us to part take in this and it was beautiful, very moving.

NOT YET

Just as I felt that thought in my mind it began to rain so we all headed inside. The time was not now, there was more that needed to happen because that could be completed. I was not even sure at this point why I was being so compelled to perform the ceremony. I wasn't even sure Miss Wellington would allow me to do it, it might come across as a little cuckoo!

IT WILL SHIFT WHAT NEEDS TO BE SHIFTED

Messages do not always come in clear, and you can drive yourself crazy overthinking everything. This is how my intuition works for me, my gifts come in vision and in "whispers". The difficult part is deciphering what is truly a channel and what is your own ego or desire. This is why I dedicated years to study and learn the techniques and ways of both the old and the new. When you work with clients you must know how to shut down your own person and ego to receive the highest and greatest good for the client. It's not a magic or calling in dead people like they show in the movies, at least not my technique. I connect to energy, pure and intentional to receive guidance and deliver results to the highest benefit of my client. Be it good or difficult messages, it is always spot on and for the best.

We continued to talk and learn from Coach as she took us through learning how to pitch yourself in sixty seconds, mingling with Natasha Mayne, a prominent, radiant powerful attorney in the Miami area. It was a different kind learning in these rooms, when a person has reached the levels that these women have seen and coming from very humble beginnings, it changes the why your mind processes. You can see yourself within them and know it is possible, everything you want is possible, "This is real, and I can have this." A mantra Stormy speaks often. She then took us to her hotel suite, and we got to witness her and the team behind her plan and mastermind. It was the most surreal experience, to see what goes on behind closed doors. Stormy was an open book; she is everything she portrays herself to be and continuing to become. Sheila made sure and gave me some pointers and helped me understand the process and how they did things. Coach has several people with her at all times, as she grew so did her portfolio of appointments, tasks and demands. To keep up with this at that level, around the clock team is needed. That's pretty well known and expected at this point yet, sitting in that room, watching and listening, this FELT different. The people in the room we not there because of money, getting exposure or favor, they were there because they love her. They had allegiance to her because of what she had done for them, how they had turned their life around by listening to her.

KNIGHTS OF THE ROUND TABLE

That was absolutely how it felt, a Woman King and her Knights. I went home from this event with a calm I had not yet experienced. With my second book launched and plans to go over to London, creating my own event to launch my book in my father's land, I was ready for my abundance. I had always wanted to go back to where I came from, my Celtic blood and again, the synchronicities, Stormy going back to Yoruba, me going back to the UK.

GAIA IS CALLING HER BLOOD BACK

I had been studying the indigenous people, the history of the Black, Indian and Latino migration prior to the colonization by the white people. Part of what many of us in this time had begun to realize is that we are in another reset, a time of "biblical" end of times, as they say. For thousands of years, we have killed and conquered, shut down the voices of the ancestors' forcing views and religions unto the people of the land, raping and killing them and making them slaves. This has been ongoing, the genocide of a people just for the riches of the Kingdom, thinking on color is better than another. Controlling the masses under fear and persecution, and turning that concept into their Church, fear God of burn in Hell forever you wretched soul. That is not God, that is not why we came here, and it is time to give back the land to the people whose blood was spilled in order to claim it. Energetically speaking, this means to set foot upon the lands of your mothers and fathers, to honor that place in which your lineage rose from. The Earth is fuel and sustenance to life, and we are the caretakers and "batteries" to her survival. Each of us has a land and a place which will trigger our very DNA to rise and come "online" to fulfill our own purpose, our own prophecy to that lineage. We are living in times of possibility where we are sophisticated enough to understand unity is the only way through this.

That is what I felt in this community, unity and breaking ancestral block and contracts of death and sorrow. Giving strength to the women who had given up on a better life, showing men they can have compassion and still be Kings. Stormy built this community because she did not have one when she was trying to step into a new path, a new trajectory, one where she would never be broke again. Never to break under the labels the World set on her, foster kid, stripper, teen mom, high school dropout, a statistic. She was commanding her own labels and by her stepping into this, she was also creating a frequency, a new vibration, she was the voice for her own self and IS the voice for this new Earth.

This time as I headed home, my head was held high, my heart was full and I was going to continue to fulfill MY dreams. To speak on stage in London, I had started the planning, worked on locations, spoke to members of the community and my social media friends who lived there. To expand the Total Life Changes products Coach had been so successful with and products that assisted me in a healthy body, expand my presence and continue the ripple effect of eradicating suicide. Christmas in London, the home of my father, my ancestral lands, to connect with cousins I had never met, to connect with sisters in the community, to CONNECT!

The one thing that has led me to my goals has always been my tenacity, and Tenacious T was back, back to serve and bloom and grow…because of her. Her sacrifice of years of building, waking every day and getting on those calls, getting in those rooms, when no one was there to support her and she was doing it all on her own, never giving up. Building not an empire, but a kingdom of love that spoke to the broken hearted who remain unbreakable.

Chapter VIII
Standing in the Eye of the Storm

London had proven to be one of the most successful endeavors, tears fell as I had landed, overwhelmed with the reality of this achievement. I had found the perfect theater in the beautiful SOHO Sanctum Hotel and the spirit of my son was with me. Signs and synchronicities aligned and as I spoke in front of my friends and family, I could feel the alchemy of the word working its magic.

Maybe it was the magic of the Christmas lights on the London streets, maybe it was the people who came to support and share love, but the surety of my path was confirmed on this trip, I was asked to be a general for the Girl Hold My Hand community. Calling members, welcoming new ones, leading the group in an occasional mediation on the morning zoom, posting clips of coach on the site. Serving as we would any church or organization, giving of my time and effort into seeds that would grow. I closed out 2023 making six figures and was able to speak on five stages and a dozen podcasts. I had several private clients working with me on their soul, the guidance offered through my metaphysical practices and my signature house clearing was also becoming a regular practice. My methods were very different from the standards known. Having been trained by the Masters at Delphi, they specialized in higher energy work, and also encouraged you to tap into your ancient knowledge and what felt right. They had been trained by generations of light workers not sages or "witches" but actual alchemists, the most famous being Patricia Hayes, Arthor Ford and Mauricio Panisset. I was fortunate enough to be trained by Mauricio's wife before she retired and some of the other children and friends of the originals. Light pushes out dark, the use of sage and incense are beautiful practices, but the heavy work is done with energy and that is my talent, infusing someone with their higher power and getting the answers they need from a session. 2023 also showed me what I continued not to need, dropping people in my life that were toxic, or that did not have my best interests. Forgiving myself for the choices that resulted in more financial hardships and let go of those failures. As you elevate, you must eliminate. I was ready for 2024, the World was continuing to spiral, we had discovered what Covid was all about, the agenda of control and keep us distracted and sick. The political conflict, the religious conflict, the race conflict, America heading into a deep separation and civil discord. Increased homeless, more starving families, drug overdose and fentanyl up forty-five percent and seventy percent of those due to fentanyl poisoning. Small businesses closing, big box corporations thriving, pharmaceutical companies making over a billion dollars with their vaccines and chronic illnesses. Vaccines that are free yet when they leave you sick and damaged and needing more medication, it costs the people not the companies. Many major players jumping on board the gravy train and endorsing this push without care to the people. We have been desensitized by the increase in violent and sexual entertainment, separated by social media and forgotten by the uber rich and wealthy. The seven deadly sins in full effect, Pride, Greed, Lust, Envy, Gluttony, Wrath, Sloth. Worshiping the celebrity, the politicians, the influencers instead of loving thyself and they neighbor. Genocides, natural disasters, moral decline, persecution of those who believe differently, global unrest, we are truly living in the end of times and the start of the new. and that meant stepping it up even more. Stormy continued to gain abundance, attention, ascension on all levels yet not without challenge. This is what truly made her so unique, she shared with the group some of her business challenges, her staff issues and how she delt with it all.

Her organization was susceptible to the same issues anyone's business, she had haters, people who left once they made it, loyalty and consistency was rare in all parts of business. Watching her deal with these situations and still expand was an immeasurable privilege. Multi-millionaires just don't share like this, and she did it because she cares about her people. She DOES it because of the calling deep within, she knows her voice will wake others to the new frequency, the frequency of wanting others to do better.

FIRST LEADER

She was that, without question. Her suffering and walk through the fire of pain to escape the program, the "matrix" as some call it and execute the creation of a frequency completely unique to our World. This is what the shift is all about. A time in which humans have a deep understanding of energy, science, esoteric, metaphysic, physical, principle and more importantly, real love of self.

In order for the meek to inherit the Earth, they must stand up and bare their sword of light that now sparks with the voice of God within their chest. For the clock of darkness will only be taken down by the chose and the chosen are ready to fight for it!

March 22, 2024 would mark the thirteenth anniversary of my sons passing. He will have been gone as long as he was alive. Several years ago I started doing incredible things on that date, so that I could slowly transmute the trauma within the memory cells of my body. It is not enough to work on thought, you must make physical action to bring in joy and erase the memory of agony and pain. I would schedule a trip with the boys, a photoshoot for a magazine, a speaking engagement or special dinner with friends. This is though, thirteen years…

Thirteen Summers to play in the shade of the trees
Thirteen Christmases for read you a story
Thirteen Halloweens to dress up with you
Thirteen Birthdays to blow out your candles
Thirteen Turkey and gravy Thanksgiving feasts
Thirteen Winters of hot chocolates

One day when you took your first breathe
One day when you took your last

...and I held you for all of them

It needed to be significant; I needed to honor him like I had never before. I always related Archangel Metatron to my Jason. Archangel Metatron is a significant figure in various religious and spiritual traditions. He is considered the highest ranking of angels, the scribe, the record keeper and some believe him to be Enoch as well. In sacred geometry, the shape that represents the structure of the Universe is Metatron's Cube which is also the base of the Star of David. Metatron's cube has thirteen circles, representing the flower of life. The two together are unity, balance and the interconnectedness of all life. I would have a special tattoo artist design and ink me the tattoo of Metatron's cube.

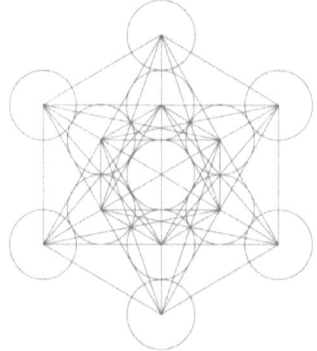

I had already found the artist, Belle Amarosa in our community owner the Las Vegas Tattoo Company, the first legal tattoo parlor in Las Vegas with the infamous Doc Baker. Belle and Doc had moved the company to Tampa many years before and their son, Colt Baker had now become an extremely successful second-generation artist. Belle was the Country's leading body piercing expert and she had been instrumental in body piercing regulations, her contributions have been significant in shaping the safety and standards. They ran the business as a family and she and Colt had seen Stormy Wellington speak on Grant Cardone's stage a few years before and of course felt the shift and the significance.

Colt, devilishly handsome and extremely talented, like my Jason, so I knew it was the perfect fit. Colt had been struggling with addiction for many years and had become a mentor and coach for many along the way. He had a recent relapse but was already out of rehab and ready to work. Who better to have then this man fighting for every day, just like me. I had meant to call Belle and discuss this all with her when she called me in early January, Colt had been found, accidental fentanyl overdose.

COLT BAKER

OMG, NO NO NO NO

My heart immediately dropped and all I could do was send everything I had to Belle and Doc.

COLT ANTHONY BAKER

The Girl Hold My Hand community came together, I went into my strength because I knew what they would need, this is what I do, I shift into the hand that will hold. Many times, I had assisted when loss of a child echoed through my path, not just in the GHMH community but anytime I heard or was asked.

You get one shot at sending your loved one-off right, you must honor YOURSELF and get it together to make it relevant for you will look back on that day many times. This was different though, I needed to fly out there, I needed to be with Belle, to help her make this everything she needed it to be. That's exactly what I did along with another sister from the community. When I flew out and looked upon her face, I saw my reflection. There is nothing like the pain of losing your child and Colt was Belle's only son. Those next few days were in service to the family, I was never more grateful for my knowledge of suffering. Because our suffering and being able to overcome, BECOMES the testimony to others. Colt was honored like a King, because a King he will always be. Belle stood tall, a true warrior and his father, having also lost a child to suicide many years before, showed up through his fog of grief and sent him off right. Belle was going to fight the war on Fentanyl, the death rate had exploded and because of its lethal strength, 100 times more potent than morphine, it only takes two milligrams to kill someone. It is estimated over two hundred deaths per day in the United States and I spoke to her about using Colt's words as she felt the rage rise within. Colt had filmed and written profound sayings on the battle of addiction; Belle herself is sober sixteen years. Before I flew back home, she had begun the planning of her first walk to fight fentanyl.

Colt's birthday was February 11, 1986 and he passed January 12, 2024. 2/11 Birth, 1/12 Death the same numbers reversed.

211
112

This became her symbol, just as 13 had become mine. The mother never wants her child forgotten so we find a way to channel our grief into purpose.

Grief is just love with no place to go

This is how we build; we build our foundations for legacy, servitudes and honor. We build on the powerful shoulders of a mother's grief. The voice of the feminine is a song of triumph as she is and always has been the true Phoenix. This holds true for the times we are in and why her leadership is key. Broken yet unbreakable and full of compassion, nurturing, and a savage who will protect beyond reason her family. As I learned more about Colt and his legacy, I found I was still called to get this tattoo and I felt if there was an artist at her studio who was close to Colt I would have him do it. Sure enough, Sweet Adam was his name and I sent him a few pictures and said, "Whatever you come up with is what it is supposed to be." I booked my flight and on March 22, 2024, two mothers came together in their resolve to keep going. They had not changed a thing in Colt's station at the shop, his dragon statues, artwork, trinkets all were there. Belle brought Colt's only daughter Bella Donna, only a toddler and for six hours I laid there for the creation Adam came up with. He combined Colt's numbers with Jasons and Archangels Metatron holding the sword of light with a J on the hilt coming through Metatron's cube. It was perfection. Everything that I represented in the essence of my son and the vibrancy of Colt's message.

Jason's baseball uniform he was cremated in, notice the logo is like the sword, the second picture is how the sunlight shows up in a picture in my back yard when I feel my son with me. A sword of light.

A sword of light.

Adam had not seen the picture of Jason in his uniform or the sword of light picture. I had no doubt Colt worked through his fingers, even his young daughter came over a few time with colored pencils and was pretending to tattoo my arm.

She had never done that, not in the many times she had spent at the tattoo parlor, not once had she ever wanted to nor approach anyone pretending to work on them.

I flew back the next day and two weeks later I was in Miami for Stormy's Awakening Intensive event, a more intimate setting of only 50 of us over three days. It was so needed for me in that moment. March had been filled with so many beautiful highs, but the lows pushed at that door of suicide again. I had closed several transactions and was in line to break one of my own records this year and then boom, things began to shift in the market. The IRS grabbed a hold of funds because of a clerical error from 2020 and I had begun to have an unexplained pain run down my right hip and thigh. I pride myself on health and fitness, having seen both my parents suffer from heart disease and obesity, my sister die from acute alcohol poisoning, my brother of cancer, I had focus my entire life on gut health and movement. At 52, I was able to keep up with the young folks in their 20s and this pain was slowing me down. Age was not something I wanted to deal with, I did not have time to slow down as there was so much more to achieve. I had lost another audition to get back on The Great American Speak off along with the smaller speak offs I was trying out for. I could not understand why my message wasn't hitting. Suicide was a hard topic to cover in 60 to 120 seconds. I had saving for my Diamond Elite ticket, and I felt confident that the deals I had would close and being in the room with her, there was a power in her presence that lifted and ignited, being with my sisters in the community, the family I had lost was now filled with these men and women. This Awakening was going to take place April 5, 6 and 7th and I knew I had to be there. Just as I knew the first time I looked into her eyes, there was a pull from my heart that was undeniable.

WASHING OF THE FEET

Yes, I would look for the opportunity to do this ceremony, it was part of the vision. I then remembered there was going to be an eclipse on April 8th, one that we had not seen with this planet alignment in over five thousand years. This eclipse has drawn comparisons to the biblical story of Jonah, who spent three days in the belly of a whale before being released in Nineveh. Interestingly, the eclipse's path of totality is set to cross over seven cities named Nineveh across the United States, sparking discussions about potential biblical connections and prophecies. We put weight to these astrological shifts and events because the most successful people in history and current billionaires all use numerology and astrology when making big decisions and choices. Another place the bible contradicts itself, Isaiah 47:13-14 warns of seeking out readers of the stars and profits. Yet Daniel interpreted dreams and had visions for which the book of Revelations, Isaiah mentions celestial events and used metaphors to prophecy over others. Elijah is another revered profit who had visions and the ability to "hear" God. These are all psychic, intuitive developed gifts, even the birth of Yeshua has the wise men follow the star to the baby. This was significant so I had to be there. It was not long before the

Awakening that Stormy announced she was also going to the 10X Growth con literally the three days prior to her event and she had a couple of private experiences with her that she was putting up. The opportunity to sit with her and dine with her all three days and have a private dinner with her for a few grand. Knowing I needed to find the opportunity to make this happen, I was one of the first to swipe up the ticket. I was headed to Miami a week early and this time it was for an even higher purpose. It stressed the savings, but knowing what was in store I knew it would come back to me in a different way. That is what she taught us, seed into what feeds you. Reciprocity, the way you do one thing is the way you do everything. If I wanted people to seed into to me, I needed to seed into them. Seeding others with a sense of responsibility toward their community. Once again, I packed my best clothes, centered myself, upgraded my seat, upgraded my room, this was going to be an epic adventure!

The first few days at Growth con with Stormy was different, she was more relaxed and feminine, she had found a deep connection and love with her boyfriend OG Boobie Black and her divine feminine grace was in every move she made. We watched the event together and spoke on the guests they had, mingled at the cocktail parties and got to meet so many people who just walked right up to you because of being there with her. She then decided to surprise myself and the other community sister to her and OG's one year Anniversary dinner and a private invitation to a new perfume launch at Sacks Fifth Avenue. She wanted us to feel the energy of wealth, not just money but WEALTH. When you become familiar with the flow of something you can begin to imagine it all the more deeply. Manifestation delivered through the sights and sounds of standing in the middle of it. During the fragrance launch, Stormy pulled me aside and handed me a custom Girl Hold My Hand Necklace with tiny pink diamonds and an engraved medallion.

"This is one of two that I had made for me, this is my personal Girl Hold My Hand necklace. I wanted to thank you for proving to me that I can reach white woman." She proudly said as she put it around my neck.

I remember Sheila taking a picture with my camera and hugging her saying, "I am never going to take this off.", I had never felt as honored as I did receive that. It was very personal for me. I had worked hard over the last year and a half to earn, serve and pay my way because I loved being here. This woman and this group of people had literally breathed life back into my broken mind and soul.

Dining at one of her favorite restaurants and watching her and OG celebrate their one year, laughing with her, having her tell me she did not know if she could have gone through what I did losing my child, those moments are priceless and this is why they say, "Get in the Room." Its not about trying to get favors, its not about being noticed as much as its about feeling the energy, learning how she moves and makes choices, it's a front row seat into what is possible. If she can do it so can I.

WASHING OF THE FEET

Diamond day would be the 7th, on a Sunday and my vision of washing her feet had been on a ship so I again, I was feeling the pull to fulfill this mission. As we headed out on Miss Wellington's yacht, mingling with the other Diamond Elite Women, I felt so grateful to have found them. Stormy had brought Sybrina Fulton, Trayvon Martin's mom. The young boy who was shot down by an angry white man and he got away with it. To not only lose your child but to have his murderer out there scot-free, making money off his book on killing a young black boy. I had barely made it through my son killing himself I don't think I could rest with his murderer still breathing. She had been organizing a yearly retreat called Circle of Mother's where her team pays for all the expenses for a mother who has lost a child violently to rest and heal. The only pledge they ask is if you return the next year and pay because that's how they fund it. Stormy made it possible for Belle and I to go to this year's retreat at the end of the month, it was another gift she gave me.

As we headed out into the water, something we did not get to do last time because of the weather, I went onto the front deck and did my qigong work. A series of slow but powerful movements that place a strong emphasis on internal energy and mental focus. Qigong uses a variety of movements and methods where something like Tai Chi is very specific. Qigong allows the movements to rise from within and flow the "chi" or life force of the Universe. I was asking for the right moment, the guidance and the anointed blessing to perform the ceremony. As the evening wore down, celebrating us at a yacht club where we pulled up in her ship and walked into the restaurant from the boat. Breaking bread with twenty other successful business men and women, millionaires to rising millionaires I was ready to ask her to allow me to do something special. Heading back to the home dock I knew I had but a few minutes to make this happen.

"Coach, I want to ask you to allow me to do something of honor for you."

She looked at me for a moment, exhausted from leading the event and being the final day. "Yes, lets get parked at the dock and then you can do what you need to do."

I quickly grabbed the roses I brought on board, roses she presented to Belle and I during the introduction to Sybrina Fulton. Roses have the highest frequency of love and these had been seeded into me so the significance of using them in the ceremony was palatable. Normally you have a large bowl of water and you place flowers and crystal in the water and wash the head, hands and feet.

There was not time for that.

I found a large sauté pan and took a bottle of water and poured it in just as we docked. I quickly announced to everyone on board

"Please everyone, I would like to do something special here tonight, something sacred."

Sheila was looking at me funny because she knew how tired Coach was and it was time to end the night. Vanessa, Stomry's personal assistant really looked at me because it was her job to keep everything running smooth and also on schedule. I looked at them both and said, "Give me a moment, this is powerful."

Coach was sitting on the edge of the dining table, her feet already bare and I began to give each person some of the rose petals from the flowers.

"In ancient times, one Queen would wash the feet of another in a sign of honor and blessing."

Suddenly I felt the channel, the reason for the ceremony and what needed to be said.

"Please turn off your phones and cameras, this is not a place nor time for technology. Tomorrow is a powerful eclipse, one that we have not seen the likes of for almost 5000 years. The alignment of the planets and the trajectory are of biblical per portion. I would ask all of you, to bless your Queen and add those rose petals to this water so that she may continue this journey."

Everyone shut their phones down and added their petals to the pan of water. I then knelt at her feet and began washing her feet with my hands.

"For the sins of the white flesh that has persecuted the black, may this be washed from our ancestry. For the strength and energy to continue to be a FIRST LEADER, to radiate and reach the women in this World who need to hear your voice of all color. We honor you; we love you. As above, so below, and so it is."

I understood it now, clearing the ancient dark energy of what my race had done to hers. It had nothing to do with my direct family or lineage, it was the call of the Universe asking for someone to step up and be the one. The one to begin the ripple effect, the tiny spark of clearing this karma from all of our lines of family and past lives. Blood may be thicker than water, but LOVE is thicker than blood. A frequency of anointing the blood for this Woman King to walk this path and receive all that she deserves and desires through her heart of hearts leading a new way.

The next morning was Monday and tapping into the morning meditation with the community felt very different, April 8th was the day of the solar eclipse and Coach spoke on this during the meditation. A few women texted me about not being correct about the eclipse because we have eclipses all the time and I tried to explain it was the path and the alignment of planets that made it rare.

PREPARE YOURSELF, WHEN SIGNIFICANT MESSURES ARE MADE TO ENLIGHTEN, THE DARK WILL COME FOR YOU

Yes, I needed to recognize this path is not for the weak, this was why it had to be me. I chose to be the one to eradicate suicide from my life which meant I was strong enough to also be a messenger and speak my truth regardless of the criticism. I was due to fly back to Arizona, I had been in Miami a week and felt so complete. I dressed in one of the outfits I had purchased from Stomry's Boutique and had a beautiful lunch on the ocean as I watched the Eclipse. I felt it, significantly, and as I travelled home others could feel it on me as well. I was upgraded automatically on each flight to first class and my frequent flyer lounges had the perfect tables and quick service. Conversations I had with others and the energy radiating from my person was palatable.

This is what happens with you move beyond faith and into knowing. IT IS FELT and sustainable. This is why we gather, why we get into the rooms, to share and exchange our knowing and rise. The next Awakening Intensive would be in July, the regular influence of these events kept me grounded and centered but I also felt the longing to advance my certifications at Delphi and go back to the special place and teachers that had given me the first gift of knowing. Having fulfilled the vision from that mediation years before, it was time to return. The color and sound training would take place in June but that pain in my hip and right leg was getting worse. I could no longer do my beloved yoga and hiking without both legs getting weak and it was now taking several minutes upon waking just to stand without pain. I finally broke down and got an MRI in May. What it showed was completely unexpected and I could not wrap my head around how this could be happening now.

The MRI showed severe facet arthritis disease of the lowest vertebra above the tail bone, cysts inside the vertebrae and the disk had completely de-hooded and slipped out. The condition was rapidly deteriorating and when I would lay down or sleep, the damaged bone would slip back and cut of the spinal cord from the waist down. The only option was surgery or slowly lose my control from the waste down. Each day it would get a little worse, a little more painful but I pushed through. I began to take intense care of my body, fortifying it, resting, real estate transactions were still happening, but the market was headed for a stagnancy, I had planned on launching a module to help others overcoming suffering and the added certification in color and sound would expand my expertise, but work was slow. People and the World was dipping further into the end times, and I was never more sure of the repair of our past ancestorial karmas to bring us together.

I continued my duties as a general in the community, leading some of the meditations, supporting coach where I could but the pain could no longer be ignored and just before leaving for Delphi in June I met with a highly recommended surgeon. He explained at length the procedure, it was going to take a year to recover, at least three months of a cane and walker and six months before flying and working out again. So many things could go wrong and the date he had available for this major surgery would be right before the next Awakening. WHY! I had done everything I was led to, sacrificed, fought, built, expanded, invested into becoming this version of myself only to be blind-sided and physically completely shut down.

PREPARE YOURSELF, WHEN SIGNIFICANT MESSURES ARE MADE TO ENLIGHTEN, THE DARK WILL~~TH~~ COME FOR YOU

I had no choice, the longer I went without the surgery, the worse the symptoms were becoming. I made it to Delphi for the week ling course and reenergized my spirit and worked on the etheric body strength. The etheric body is believed to be responsible for the flow of energy within the body and can influence health, emotional well-being and spiritual development. While we have seen spontaneous healings and miracles in this field, I also understand that the body will have issues as time passes. Returning from Delphi I was at the pinnacle of calm and certainty I could make it through this and the time of healing I could produce another book, one that spoke of what Stormy had given me, given the community and soon the entire planet. I was heart sick about missing the next awakening, but I could not keep putting off the procedure as I was risking permanent damage to my spinal cord. The Great American Speak Off was having another audition virtually and at this point I had given up on these contests but something in me told me to do it just for fun. It was the same format, 60 seconds for the first and second rounds and if you made it to the final 2 minutes. You had to attend the whole day for two days to get through everyone and continue to the next rounds so you had some time to watch others and practice. The morning of the first day I suddenly changed my speech. Instead of just going straight into the incident and talking of suicide I choose to tell the other part of the story, the one where this tragedy turned me onto real estate and becoming the Country's First Metaphysical Realtor and why. It worked. I made it passed the first and second rounds and on day two, I won a Golden Ticket once again! I would be competing in January on the stage in Miami for the top three final spots at the final Growth

Con, the tenth one. I followed what Stormy has said over and over, just speak from the heart and that's what I did.

June nineteenth, Juneteenth as it is known, is a significant day for coach and we as a community see the relevance of coming together in all colors, religions, everything needs to come together for thing to change. As I sat and listened to the announcements and meditation, I heard my son

GIVE HER ONE OF MY BASEBALLS MOM

I had been thinking about my next book, what I was going to title it, how I was going to share this story, allowing it to form slowly over knowing I would be laid up for a bit. I had originally intended to tell Stormy in person about the book but now I was not going to be able to see her so hearing my son say this, on a day we celebrate the emancipation of the enslaved Black people in America, the end of slavery. Further confirmation of my purpose and the writing of this story. Suicide, suffering, inequality, economic disparities and limited access to resources compared to white people have increasingly reached critical points in the country. I thought of all the challenges I had been through from my childhood, domestic violent marriages and rapes, loss of parents, siblings and children. So many things but then I thought about what it would have been like if I was black.

What would that all have been like for me if I was black instead of this small blond, green eyed white woman?

GIVE HER ONE OF MY BASEBALLS

She needed to know that not only was my heart with hers, but the essence of my son, HIS legacy, HIS cause was also with her. To stop suffering for ALL and to have the voice of a white woman bring awareness that it is time we come together and stop all this hate. She needed to understand that her continuing to evolve, and lead would eventually be the beginning of this New Earth. She would often speak about being spiritual not religious, that she had seen so many pays in their tithings yet what did they get in return? She spoke truths and gave solutions, sometimes with authority and other times with empathy but always with love. The end of times also means a new beginning of times and this vision of unity, no one idolized or worshiped, men not above the women and the huge gap of wealth closed. The new times to come would be built on wanting the best for thy neighbor, no more hunger, providing proper health care and skill training, building businesses off what you love to do and what you create. It starts here, it starts now, by clearing the karma of our father's father and our mother's mother. I had been playing with the idea of the title as I said and just then it came, both the vision of the cover and the title, because that is exactly where I was standing in the moment. The calm space in the eye of the storm and the storm was Stormy Wellington. She was the calm, she had given me back my drive, my desire to try, my ability to see possibilities again and confirmation of my deeper knowing and that I was not insane.

It is through the black woman that we would see this paradise on earth delivered for there is not greater sorrow then in the DNA of the black woman. Her people, her children, theirs is the scream of the forgotten and mistreated for millennia. It is their skin in which the melanin of God sings for their color was the first color and the one most deeply connected to magic of the soil of the Earth. *Black Girl Magic*

I decided to write her a note and wrapped the baseball and sent it to Sheila Woodward to give to her at the right time. I then worked on the book cover and sent it to Coach letting her know what I was working on and then I began to write.

A few days later Sheila called, "Kim, you must be there, Coach shared the title of the book with me. I think you should be the one to give her the baseball and get to the awakening."
"Sheila, I have my surgery scheduled and I really can't put it off any longer." I replied
I sat there for a moment, "Let me call the surgeons office and see if they have something for the day after I would get back from Miami."

Sure enough, they did, I could push through this next few weeks, I could make it. The next Awakening intensive was July 12, 13, 14, and 15th with the surgery set for the 17th. I had been following a strict supplement and food protocol for the best outcome and I could stick to it while traveling. The challenge would be only Tylenol for the pain, but I was all I was using at that time plus steroids. The steroids had already been eliminated so natural breath work, cold plunge, energy clearing was all I had either way to address it. June 30th, I got a call from Dr Mark Wang's office, Dr Wang was a surgeon I had tried to get in to see but he had been completely booked and I wasn't even sure if his technique would work on my situation. He was young and innovative in the spinal surgery field. I had seen a good handful of information and videos on laparoscopic type techniques, eliminating having to go through the full ten-inch incision and filet open the muscles in the back to allow full access to the spine. It was preferred to have full access to be sure the removal of the diseased bone and restructure with screws, cage and plate was done with as little damage to the spinal cord as possible for obvious reasons. The laparoscopic was guided by ultrasound-like vision. Dr Wang had an opening for a quick consultation on July 10th, just one day prior to leaving for Miami and one week prior to my already scheduled surgery. I had already completed weeks' worth of blood work, x-rays and screening to show I was healthy, so I took all of that with me. He reviewed the MRI, my reports and looked at my husband and I and said yes, piece of cake he could do it, not only could he do it but he had some things he was going to do differently to give me a better result and the down time would be cut in half. Without having to do all the invasive part to access the spine, I would be able to fly and work out again in three months and be mostly recovered in six. I had excellent health besides this and there was no reason to think I would not have a full recovery. I cried a bit as we sat there letting the Dr's team know we were ready to switch and get scheduled. They were going to get me on the books as soon as they could and I focused on my trip to Miami, one last hurrah before this next challenge.

As always, the Awakening experience was all it was meant to be, Stormy growing ever more impactful and powerful, the lessons, the connections, her delivery of the WORD hit us all where it needed to. She had spoken of one of her long-time heroes, Rev. Dr. Iyanla Vanzant, an American inspirational speaker, lawyer, New Thought spiritual teacher, author, life coach, and television personality. She is known primarily for her books, her eponymous talk show, and her appearances on The Oprah Winfrey Show. She is also a Yoruba Priestess, a minister in one of the most ancient African Traditions that exists. The original alchemist. The Yoruba teach four basic principles to live by:
Principles that support a life of balance, value, and order:

Omoluwabi
A set of cultural principles that guide the Yoruba people to live a life of virtue and excellence. Omoluwabi embodies values such as integrity, respect, self-control, and empathy.

Circular cosmology

The Yoruba believe in a circular cosmology that emphasizes continuity, reciprocity, and balance between the living, the unborn, and the ancestors. The circle symbolizes eternity and the idea that each person is part of a larger community.

Justice

The Yoruba believe that justice is central to interpersonal relations. Justice is preserved through a system of mutual expectations, where society expects people to contribute to progress and stability, and individuals expect their needs to be met.

Ifa scripture

The first four principles of Ifa scripture represent the cycle of life, birth, death, and rebirth.

The Yoruba people also believe in a complex spiritual ontology, where humans exist in both the physical and spiritual worlds. They believe that a person's life is made up of three elements: the body, the soul, and the spirit.

All of the basic ideas I had studied and seen in many reigns of peace and for our future. There is a common thread in the beliefs and faiths of all religions and the core message is to love one another as we would our God and God is within. Iyanla Vanzant was there, at the Awakening, Coach had been honored by her and came to speak with us not just one day, but two! Where Stormy had the rays of the Sun surround her as she walked in and showed us her ways, Iyanla Vanzant was the Universe gliding through that door. Her wisdom, her developed sense and ability to tap in instantly was overwhelming. We all hung on every word and the shift she created for so many of us, God was heavy in that room all weekend. As I sat listening and taking note of how Stormy was also taking notes, I noticed a necklace that Iyanla was wearing, a gold chain with Metatron's cube.

JASON'S BASEBALL

Seeing the necklace and reflecting on all that had occurred, synchronicities, everything happening as it should. Sheila had received the package and held onto it and I had printed out the first eight pages I had written of the book ready to give to her. My surgery not only had been rescheduled but because of that, I was also able to see a specialist and find an even better option for me. I made it to the Awakening so I could be at my highest frequency and mindset and so I could receive the blessing of writing this book prior to going full into it. From the original vision years ago to seeing all of it come to fruition along with the many other visions of standing on stage, launching my second book, getting back into decent real estate sales to expanding my healing practice and winning another Golden Ticket, the place where all of this started me on this path to this place and this moment.

Once again, as we completed the evening on the Yacht, several of the Diamond Elites, Coach and her man OG Boobie Black, some of her best friends and team I chose to give it to her just before we disembarked the ship. I had but the baseball, one from out of his baseball bag I had saved, in a pink box, the color of the Girl Hold My Hand logo along with $211 and $13 dollars. The 211 for Colt Anthony Baker and the 13 for Jason Paul Legere. I wanted to seed into her the spirit of the children who were thankful to her for supporting their mothers. I wanted her to feel the commitment and gratitude beyond the norm, beyond the veil. She sat and read the few pages I included, and she smiled, "This is good, it grabs my attention, I can't wait to read more."

We sat there a bit longer and she gave me one last hug before we all said good night and headed back to our hotels, back to our homes and back to our lives, transformed.

I was ready for the surgery, I was ready for this book, I was ready to serve.

My life ended March 22, 2011, as my son took his last breath at age 13
Thirteen years later a Black Woman breathed life back into this broken White Woman and her purpose unfolded.

We are in a time of reset, a new beginning that will only happen when the flow of life is restored. Not the perfect paradise but one that thrives and evolves for the greater good of all not the one or the few. We are in the age of the change of times and the call for the reset has been raised. The polarities have shifted so far off balance our very existence is on the verge of extinction. There have been five major mass extinctions in Earth's history, with the most notable the extinction of the dinosaurs approximately sixty-six million years ago. The sixth extinction, however, is unique in that is largely driven by human actions rather than natural events. Science now estimates we are in an accelerated rate much higher than expected. Look around, slowly we have been desensitized and dumbed down, slowly we have gotten unhealthier, needed more pharmaceuticals, slowly we are becoming obsolete. We have been told who to be and what to do since the day we came out of the womb. Labelled and shoved into schools and programs and asked to choose one of their ways to make money and life your life instead of developing your own ideas. The World has been shaped into a masculine heavy rule and we must level the polarity. The planet has been littered, destroyed and stripped in the greed for more opulence when it's the very trees they chop down that keeps them alive. We have evolved enough to understand energy and the expansion of those gifts through science and practice. Our favorite thing to be is human and if we do not wake up to what we have done to each other and the planet we are facing the 6th Extinction. Pain is inevitable in the glorious landscape of being alive, it's the suffering that is a choice. Why are we choosing ourselves over the suffering of others? How many houses do you need? How many cars, ships, planes, buildings, shoes, clothes, bags…it never is enough, and it never ends.

The is no better place then under the shade of a tree, the breeze kissing your cheek holding the hand of a man that loves you.
There is no better place to be then sitting outside at a table, breaking bread with your friends and family.
There is no better place to be then sitting in a circle telling stories as the moon is high in the sky.
There is no better place to be than a cup of coffee in the quiet morning as the Sun rises
There is no better place to be then watching your grandchildren running on the beach as you throw the ball to your pup

We have forgotten the most precious commodity of community and time with each other, replacing it with screens and AI. We have allowed our hate and prejudices to grow and the empathy and compassion to hide behind the name of some charity that we donate to once a year. We find beauty in the sculpted perfection of someone's body instead of their skills and talents.

The World has forgotten what love is and we are calling for those leaders, the ones from that first channeled message on March 13, 2020 (there is that 13 again)

Families are forced to stay at home
Cleanse the Earth of Darkness
Bring them into love
We are the Leaders
This is your Kingdom
This is why you feel the need to travel
You are being called to lead the Chaos with love
Only those who feel the calling of love will make it through this decade
Religions and Governments will be reconstructed
The leaders who will inherit the Earth are the ones chosen by the People
The people will choose the ones who love them---and who loved them first

The Planet is dying, and calling back the blood, the clearing of the karma of the indigenous people who were slaughtered in greed

The Universe is feminine, and she is calling back her voice that has been suffocated for far too long

…and the Voice of one of the first leaders is Stormy Nicole Wellington

Now, just breathe…

Postscript

October 29, 2024

Hello My Lovelies,

I could not leave you all completely hanging on that last note regarding the surgery. It was a complete success; I am healing three times faster than normal expectations and already dancing with my swords and do my qigong again. I am still striving to make the dream come to fruition, still driving towards success and dodging those sledgehammers.

But I know what my purpose is and tonight, as I finished this book, at exactly 4:40 pm and sent Stormy a note that it was complete at 4:44pm in her 44th year, I realized today is also her tenth year as the top network marketer and builder in Total Life Changes.

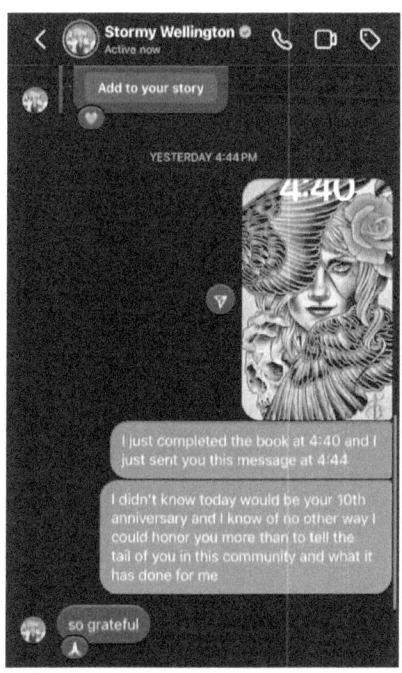

As we like to say, you can't make this shit up!

It is not what you go through, it is how you come through it.

KIMBERLY TOCCO

 *2 TIME GOLDEN TICKET 10X Stages Winner!*

HGTV Pool Hunters Real Estate Professional
iTunes First Release Original Meditation
https://music.apple.com/us/album/overcome-just-breathe/1765975881?i=1765975882
Check out my podcast: Tenacious Thoughts
https://apple.co/3frOJJ4

https://www.youtube.com/c/KimberlyTocco
Three X Published #1 Best Seller
https://www.TenaciousAngels.com
Advanced Metaphysician Certified Spiritual Psychologist
American Association of Drugless Practitioners
2024 Homeowner Magazine Humanitarian Award
2023 So Scottsdale Magazine Women to Watch
2023 Heart & Hustle Award Real Producer Magazine
2022 Certified Spiritual Healer
2021 Master Level Energy & Certified Heart Healing Practitioner
2020 Scottsdale Homeowner Magazine Humanitarian of the Year
2019 Philanthropist of the Year EXP Global Realty
2018 Most Inspiring Realtor

www.ingramcontent.com/pod-product-compliance
Lightning Source LLC
Chambersburg PA
CBHW021937160426
43195CB00011B/1121